ONE-PERSON PUPPETRY

Streamlined *&* Simplified

With
38
Folktale
Scripts

YVONNE
AMAR
FREY

American Library Association
Chicago   2005

Photos by Charles J. Frey

Stage-making diagram drawing by Ana Lyra

While extensive effort has gone into ensuring the reliability of information appearing in this book, the publisher makes no warranty, express or implied, on the accuracy or reliability of the information, and does not assume and hereby disclaims any liability to any person for any loss or damage caused by errors or omissions in this publication.

Composition and design by ALA Editions in Futura Book and Berkeley using QuarkXPress 5.0 for the PC

Printed on 50-pound white offset, a pH-neutral stock, and bound in 10-point coated cover stock by Data Reproductions

The paper used in this publication meets the minimum requirements of American National Standard for Information Sciences—Permanence of Paper for Printed Library Materials, ANSI Z39.48-1992. ∞

Library of Congress Cataloging-in-Publication Data
Frey, Yvonne Amar.
    One-person puppetry streamlined and simplified : with 38 folktale scripts /
  Yvonne Amar Frey.
        p.   cm.
    Includes bibliographical references.
    ISBN 0-8389-0889-6
    1. Puppet plays, American. 2. Puppet theater. I. Title.
    PN1980.F74 2004
    791.5'30973—dc22   2004017388

Printed in the United States of America

09   08   07   06   05   5   4   3   2   1

I dedicate this book to the memory of two Chicago educators:

my uncle, Dr. M. Benedict Amar,
who taught me a love of literature, in particular drama;

and my father, Dr. Wesley F. Amar,
who showed me how much fun performing can be.

Contents

Part Three
APPENDIXES

Introduction

*O*nce upon a time, in a land gone mad with the noise from cell phones and Walkmans, lived a middle-aged librarian who refused to grow up. She wasn't the kind of librarian who required silence in the library or one who pursed her lips and shook her finger at patrons who asked questions, spoke too loudly, or wanted to chat as they looked for material to read. No, she encouraged lively conversation and discussion. But after a full day of helping little patrons (she worked in the children's room of the library), she found herself inevitably ready to enjoy a good book at home for some peaceful, quiet, restful reading at night. Instead of making her way to the adult section of the library, where her fellow librarians chose the recent releases as reading material, however, she'd usually make a final pass through the J398s and bring home a good version of a fairy tale or folktale to read. She told herself this was so that she could prepare herself for the next day's story time, but really that was only half-true. You see, she truly liked these stories. She had since she was a little girl.

But how could she best share this love of fantasy with her young story-time audiences? These children had grown up, after all, with professionally acted audiotape and videotape performances of stories, fast-moving cartoons, and video games. How could she compete? She already tried to read with expression, using different voices for the characters as she read, but something was still missing. How could she get her audience more involved in the tales?

She glanced up at the library office with the Peg-Board wall filled from top to bottom with plastic-bagged puppets on hooks, ready to use for the monthly library puppet performances she did with another librarian. It was a shame that those cute puppets had to be sealed away for the rest of the month. As if by magic—poof!—she had it. The answer was right in front of her. She looked at those expressive little papier-mâché faces grinning at her from inside their bags. Maybe there was one easy way to enliven her storytelling, a different way to tell stories of a simpler, richer world of imagination and enchantment without any audiovisual assistance. Help was close by. She would write the fairy tales and folktales into scripts for puppet shows, but these would be short, simple shows she could perform by herself. She would forgo the props, the large wooden puppet stage, and the *help of a fellow puppeteer. Could she do it alone? Well, she wouldn't really be alone. She'd have the help of all of those puppets, who seemed more than ready to be released from their confinement. They lived for performing, after all.*

I don't remember when I was first introduced to puppetry. I grew up in an extended family in which there was always an adult lap to crawl into for a story. My dad had been born and raised in the South, and he regularly read Uncle Remus stories to my brother and me, using the original dialect written by Joel Chandler Harris. We were always encouraged to use our imaginations and to write stories and stage small plays, play piano, make creative crafts, and entertain the rest of the family. When I was old enough to read by myself, I haunted the fairy-tale section of our public library. Of course we didn't have the DVDs, CDs, videos, and games available today, but we did have good books to read as well as good children's television shows that featured puppets to watch, like the *Kukla, Fran and Ollie Show, Howdy Doody,* and the *Buster Brown Show,* with a very naughty Froggie that always finished everyone else's sentences with an inappropriate and funny remark. Once a year, my parents would treat us to the extravagantly staged puppet performances at Kungsholm, a dinner theater in Chicago that staged a number of complete operas with ornately attired puppets manipulated under the stage floor for all the roles of the opera. The opera part never impressed me as much as those beautiful puppets. They were fascinating to watch. It was those elegant, elaborate performances of puppet operas that I thought of when I was asked years later what I knew about puppetry during a job interview for my first children's librarian job, at Peoria Public Library in Peoria, Illinois. The children's librarians, after all, were accustomed to performing several puppet shows each month in the large library auditorium. "Would you be able to stage regular puppet shows?" the library director, Alex Crossman, asked me.

Full puppet shows on a regular schedule? I came to children's librarianship as a second career, having taught English literature for a number of years in college and high school. I had been in charge of speech and drama in my high school teaching, and had directed musicals and other plays, but this was something very different, and it was a little frightening. None of my classes in library school had prepared me for this. I think that I must have answered the director's question a little hesitantly: "I'd be willing to try." One of the most unsettling aspects of puppetry then for me was that instead of having the safe vantage point of being a play director, I would now be an actor—one of two hardworking puppeteers responsible for the whole show and onstage every second of the play. I knew the amount of work involved in putting on the yearly high school musical. Would puppetry demand this same amount of work every month?

Little did I know then that puppetry would become one of my passions. Luckily for me, the director was willing to take a chance on me. It was also fortunate that the library already had a well-established puppet script collection ready to perform, a large collection of papier-mâché handmade puppets, and a large, custom-built wooden puppet stage. The head of the children's department, an experienced puppeteer, Lee Olsson, took me under her wing and taught me the basics for our monthly puppet shows. I quickly found out, however, that to be a puppeteer takes more than reading the puppet scripts behind the stage and moving the puppets around a little. Reading books about puppetry might be a start, so I brushed up by reading some books. I soon discovered, however, that many skills just have to be practiced in order to be mastered: skills like reading the scripts with expression; speaking slowly enough and projecting loudly enough to be clearly understood; listening for and responding to the audience's reactions; writing lines of humor into the scripts to appeal to the young audience members; pacing the shows so that the total performance time is not too long for the attention span of the young; keeping individual puppet scripts uncluttered and short; allowing the puppet who is speaking to move and gesture while keeping the other ones still; reading and performing with a fellow puppeteer, and anticipating the lines of the other, or ad-libbing if your partner makes a mistake and the lines are not delivered as the script reads; interspersing the short plays with participatory songs or brief pieces of entertainment performed in front of the stage; and manipulating puppets on both of your hands in believable motions and gestures even though you cannot see what they are doing and your arms and wrists are getting tired.

Two of us, both librarians in the children's department, performed a selection of three or four puppet scripts each month in back of the wooden stage in the auditorium. Because we were using a traditional puppet stage, we crouched on stools or chairs in back of the stage. During the entire show, we had to keep our arms extended above our heads while we manipulated the puppets. We went home after a show with aching arms and shoulders. (I'm afraid that my puppets may have sagged a bit during the performance of a long play.) This was wonderful puppetry training, however, even if it was fatiguing. I had lots of practice in ad-libbing, projecting my voice, delivering lines expressively, and, especially, manipulating the puppets' action by feel rather than by sight.

Despite the sore arm muscles, I gradually found that I looked forward to those monthly shows in the library auditorium. I could really exaggerate my lines, and the audience responded with attention and delighted laughter. I could be silly onstage and hide my embarrassment behind the figure of my puppet character. Our audience attendance started to grow as we got better and more polished. I began to write more puppet scripts from new picture books that were added to the collection. (At this time we didn't worry too much about copyright.) I also started creating more puppets from papier-mâché, as the scripts demanded different puppet characters. After a few months, when the head of the children's department retired, I was now the most experienced puppeteer in the library.

As the demands of running the children's room grew, I found that I had less and less time to practice with another librarian for the puppet shows. (It is necessary to have at least one or two practices together for the show to run smoothly.) Also, having two librarians performing the puppet shows in the auditorium on a Saturday afternoon meant that there was less help available for staffing the children's room circulation desk at the busiest time of the week. But our audiences were growing for the monthly show, so we continued to perform two-person puppet shows once every month.

Before summer reading programs started, the children's librarians visited each school to encourage attendance in the library's summer program. Instead of simply speaking before the school body from the stage and passing out materials, I decided to write a puppet script I could perform. Not knowing any other way to do puppetry, I hoisted that huge wooden stage on top of my car and carried it into the school auditoriums. After a few performances, my whole body—not just my shoulders and arms—ached. These summer puppet shows were the first times I had attempted to perform puppetry without the help of a second puppeteer, and I learned quickly the things to do and not to do to make the shows better and less exhausting when I was working alone.

I discovered that some of the techniques I had learned in two-person puppetry did not work when I performed a one-person show. First, some of the scripts that worked so well for our two-person shows required multiple puppet characters and quick changes. I soon learned how difficult and frustrating it was to take off one puppet character and replace it with another during the course of a scene, especially with another puppet character already on your other hand. Also, many characters meant that many different voices had to be used. Of course I was not only the voice for all the characters but the voice of the narrator as well. Props were hard to manage also. I had to be careful to indicate on the script the exits and entrances as well as which puppet was used on the right hand and which on the left hand.

But once I recognized the differences between one-person puppetry and puppetry performed with two or more puppeteers and made some changes in the way I performed, I found that one-person puppetry has many advantages over two-person puppetry—advantages that more than outweigh the problems. The biggest advantage of one-person plays is that you don't have to coordinate your schedule with that of another librarian for rehearsals and performances. You can even practice at home, whenever and wherever it is convenient. Since you are performing alone, you can use a much smaller portable stage that fits on a tabletop, making it very easy to transport and store. Of course you also have the choice of performing the scripts that are your favorites as well as the flexibility of switching order or changing scripts in response to the audience's reaction. Finally, if you are charging a fee for the show, you can ask for a more reasonable rate, since you have no other puppeteer to share it with.

When I left my job in the children's room at the public library, I still wanted to continue performing with puppets. For a short time I did shows with my son as a second puppeteer and with my father performing some of the musical interludes. Gradually, however, I switched over to performing by myself.

Through the years I have modified my techniques and learned some shortcuts that can make one-person puppetry a relatively stress-free, enjoyable experience. The plays that I now write and perform are not written from picture books (so there is no copyright problem in performing them) but are original adaptations of folklore or are original stories. The scripts use the voice of a narrator who can fill in all the background information and is not a puppet figure. All of the scripts in this book are written for one person to perform with a minimum of puppet changes. Most of the scripts are written for just two puppet characters, so quick changes backstage are unnecessary. Although it is difficult, if not impossible, for one person to perform the traditional story lines for tales like "The Three Billy Goats Gruff" or "The Three Little Pigs," which normally have four major characters, the scripts in this book are based upon rewritten tales that use two major characters. In the script retelling of "The Three Billy Goats Gruff" in this book, for example, the action of the play involves only one Billy Goat and one troll. (Because these are adaptations of the traditional tales, teachers might also use the scripts as springboards for studying the traditional story or as models for creative writing.)

I have also learned to keep props to a minimum. In most cases, if one prop is needed, it can simply be placed onstage before the play begins. In many plays no props need to be used at all. Remember that since you are moving the puppets in front of the curtain and cannot see the actions of the puppets, it is difficult to have the puppets navigate around a lot of props or carry or move props. Sometimes, if a small prop is needed for the play, you can simply pin or attach the prop to the character—for example, pinning a letter to the hand of a puppet.

This book is geared toward the amateur puppeteer—the librarian or teacher or parent who wants to explore this form of reaching out to children but who doesn't necessarily have a lot of time or resources.

Having been both a librarian and a classroom teacher, I realize how limited time is for embarking on a project like puppetry. The task may seem costly and overwhelming, considering making puppets, constructing a stage, writing or adapting scripts, and practicing and performing the plays. Just reading over this list may be discouraging.

Don't be discouraged. Throughout the book I will explain shortcuts you can take to still have the fun and experience of one-person puppetry without many of the expensive and time-consuming aspects of performance. In chapter 1 I show why the imaginative release that puppetry provides is important to a child's literary development as well as how teachers, librarians, and even parents can use these techniques in the classroom, library, and the home.

In chapter 2 I provide tips on how to create your own puppets and portable puppet stage easily and very inexpensively. You can create the simple stage I suggest from a large carton, or you can perform the scripts without the use of a stage. In the third chapter, I provide some performance tips that will help even the inhibited puppeteer have success.

My simplified method may go against some of the established suggestions that you will find in other books on puppetry, even some listed in my bibliography. I have found through years of practice, however, that this method is an effective alternative to some of the more established ways of performing puppet shows, particularly if you are doing one-person plays. Some of the basic differences between my approach and others I have read about follow:

- scripts are short—requiring about five to eight minutes of performing time;
- emphasis is on the language and the voices of the puppets instead of on action;
- plot details are filled in by the narrator voice, which is used more extensively than it would be used if there were more than two characters in the plays;
- hand and glove puppets are in large part created in minutes from stuffed toys or are fashioned with papier-mâché heads;
- the performance stage—created from a cardboard carton—is light and portable;
- scripts are attached to the curtain with Velcro so that the puppeteer does not need to memorize lines; and
- puppets perform in front of the curtain, allowing the puppeteer to reach under the curtain with the puppets on his or her hands and to be seated in a more comfortable position during the performance.

I don't claim to be a professional puppeteer. I am an amateur puppeteer–librarian who makes puppets and stages, writes scripts for the shows, and performs them for various groups. Although I like to perform before a group, I don't like to trust my memory for all the script lines. (That might be the major reason I would much rather direct a play than act in it.)

I suspect that there are more teachers and librarians like me who would like to perform puppetry but think that they could never do it—maybe because it is too costly, too time-consuming, or that it requires an uninhibited dramatic person with a phenomenal memory. One-person puppetry does not have to be any of those things. This method of performing one-person shows can be a painless yet very effective way for librarians, classroom teachers, and parents (homeschoolers or others) to incorporate puppetry into their curriculum and into their programs. Although it is true that more preparation and materials are needed for performing puppetry than for other forms of storytelling, it is also true that if you use some of the ideas in this book for creating puppets, making your stage, and performing the scripts, you can readily and inexpensively perform one-person puppet shows. It may surprise you to discover the delighted reactions from your young audiences, the smiles, laughter, and even cheers, which will reward your extra efforts.

Part One

TIPS AND TECHNIQUES FOR THE PUPPETEER

Chapter 1

Why Perform Puppet Shows?

*T*here's something magical about a puppet show. Even after performing many puppet shows through the years, I am always amazed to rediscover how open children are to fantasy—how ready and eager they are to suspend their disbelief and enter into the realm of make-believe that a puppet show envelops them in. Staging one puppet show or even using a puppet on your arm during a story time will convince you of this. If a group is fidgety or noisy before you begin, simply bring out a puppet on your arm—instant quiet and instant attention. All eyes will be on the puppet and not on you as the speaker. Even older students happily enter into the fun. I have had fourth graders line up for a handshake from one of the puppets after the show, for example. One preschool child in an audience asked me once where the puppets go and what they do when they aren't performing. I must admit that I have been curious about that myself.

You do not need to use the most expensive and realistic puppets or the finest props to enter into the fun. In fact, I think that in some ways the more homey and simple the props and puppets are, the easier it is for the child to use his or her own imagination and escape into the fantasy (see chapter 2 for tips on making your own puppets).

But what makes puppet shows a special form of storytelling for children? Puppet shows, like many good children's books, provide a mirror for children to see themselves in, often using animal characters to depict real human dilemmas—the types of situations and problems in which the children in the audience may find themselves. Somehow, it feels safe, less threatening, for the child to watch a puppet character deal with these problems. The child can vicariously "test the waters." For example, a child may, like Goldi Locks in the play in this book, be lonely and wish to have more friends to play with. The child can observe a puppet character dealing with the problem of loneliness by trying various techniques to make friends. Some of the puppet character's tactics may work, some may not, but the child in the audience learns that others may have the same problems he or she has and that not every solution works. Ultimately, the child may discover some new tactics for making friends that just might work. That is not to say that a major component of the puppet shows is to teach behavior—in fact, the quickest way to turn off a child's interest in a show is to become too didactic. However, often the child viewing the puppet show can rather easily intuit a suggested moral or lesson to be learned during the course of the show.

Puppetry can also help the child in developing communication skills, listening skills, and literary analysis skills. Whether the child is performing in a puppet show or is listening to a show being modeled by a teacher or librarian, he or she learns the importance of talking loudly enough to be heard, enunciating clearly, speaking expressively, and talking at a rate that the audience can understand. During a puppet play, children quickly learn that they must listen carefully, as the humor of the situation often comes about when one of the puppet characters misunderstands the other. Since the puppet script is so short, the child in the audience has to concentrate in order to follow the actions and the dialogue.

From the librarian or teacher's standpoint, the puppet script also is a unique, entertaining way to introduce children to literature. Through the puppet play, children learn all the elements of a story. The script is simple but with an identifiable beginning, middle, and end. Some conflicts or complications in the plot allow the action to advance. Usually the characters are not fully rounded because of the limitations of time, but the characters do possess certain recognizable traits or characteristics, and the action that results is compatible with those character traits. Even though the child willingly enters into the fantasy of the play, the characters and action and the language have to be believable enough so that the audience can easily enter into the spirit of the play.

Often, as in good storytelling, there is a little twist to the ending of the story; however, the ending is in many cases fairly predictable, even anticipated. A puppet show often contains clear foreshadowing of action, sometimes in the form of the repeated phrase or refrain. Just as in a cumulative tale, which helps to introduce a young child to a developing sequential course of action, a repeated phrase or refrain in the puppet script often helps to punctuate the stages of the story line as the plot builds toward an anticipated ending.

If traditional folktales and fairy tales have universal appeal, and are even beneficial to a child's psychological development, as Bruno Bettelheim suggests in his *Uses of Enchantment: The Meaning and Importance of Fairy Tales* (New York: Random House, 1989), what better way to introduce these multicultural traditional tales than to present them in puppet shows? The fairy tale—with its simple action, its characters that are easily constructed, its predictable structure of the story line, its use of refrains, and its colorful language—is a natural for a puppet script, either as a retold adaptation of the original story or a modern follow-up to the traditional tale. In my view, children are entitled to the richness of their literary heritage, which is found in traditional literature. Both by listening to puppet plays written from traditional literature and by writing their own play scripts based on traditional story lines, children can obtain a better sense of their literary past and a literary background that will remain with them in their later studies in literature and reading.

Finally, involving children actively in the puppet show as puppeteers or in some other aspect of the plays can provide young students with many different channels for expressing their dramatic and artistic creativity. Even a child who might be hesitant to perform in his or her own voice may have less hesitancy in performing in the voice of a puppet. Children can engage in creative writing of their own scripts, constructing their own stages, making their own puppets, and performing their own shows. An adult librarian or teacher can use some of the materials in this book or other books on puppetry to model the various components of a puppet show. Some children in a classroom situation or library group might be more interested in the process of making the puppets, others might be more taken with the actual dramatic performance, while others might be more intrigued with writing their own scripts or retelling a fairy tale. There are many aspects of a puppet show that require choices for the students: choosing or writing the scripts, making or purchasing the puppets, constructing a stage, and finally performing the plays. This means that different aspects of puppet plays can appeal to different types of students: those who like to read, like to write, like to be artistic, and like to be dramatic. Of course there will be some students who will immerse themselves in all aspects of the puppet show. You as the teacher or librarian can allow young people to concentrate on whichever aspect or aspects of puppetry most appeal to them.

WHEN AND WHERE CAN PUPPETRY BE PERFORMED?

Whether you are a teacher, a librarian, a parent, or a grandparent, you might decide to use one-person puppetry to help you to booktalk a particular book or type of literature, to develop a theme, or to examine a concept to be learned, or you may simply want to employ puppetry as an enjoyable, entertaining break. You might, for example, want to model for students how to perform a puppet show in order to introduce them to traditional literature. For this you might choose to act out one or more of the adapted fairy tales or fables from this book. After the students see a fairy tale performed, you might then ask the class to come up with their own original retellings of a fairy tale to be written and then performed by the class as a puppet play.

Librarians and teachers can use puppetry in different ways for story times with preschool children. Instead of just reading a book yourself, you can use a puppet to read the book, or you can act out part of the text with one or two puppets. You might choose to use a puppet stage during a story time, but instead of performing several puppet scripts, you could perform a single short puppet script. The lightweight tabletop stage will work for single scripts as well as for longer programs (for tips on using puppets during story times, see the boxed text in chapter 3).

When you choose the scripts to perform, keep in mind the age of your intended audience. Children younger than three years old may have trouble sitting still for any storytelling entertainment, even puppetry. The ideal audience for puppet shows is somewhere between the ages of three and ten years old. Too young an audience may not have the necessary attention span to listen to a whole show, however short. They may also come up and pull on the performing puppets, call out to the puppets, or cry during the show. (I have had these things happen. Unfortunately, since you are in back of the curtain, you can't see the problem arising until you feel the puppet being pulled off or hear the screams.)

Even though the ideal audience for a puppet show may be a young audience, you can be lenient with the higher cutoff age. I have successfully performed shows for students in fifth and even sixth grade. Oftentimes the older students are more interested in learning how to perform the shows by themselves as well as how to write the puppet scripts. You are really modeling the art of puppetry for them.

Many times parents will also be in the audience. Try to involve them too in the play. Play up the humor in the shows, including your dramatic expressiveness and voices, to keep the parents interested as well as the younger audience. Puppetry can also be well received by adult groups in addition to children's groups. Senior citizens, for example, can enjoy puppetry, especially when the scripts are interspersed with poetry, riddles, and songs that they might know.

One-person puppetry with the small stage works best in an enclosed, quiet library room or classroom with an audience of up to fifty children who can sit around the stage table and see the actions of the puppet characters. I have tried to perform puppet shows outdoors, in very large auditoriums, and in shopping malls. In those cases, the results were exhausting and disappointing. The audience needs to be prepared to sit and concentrate on the lines of the plays—not wander around. Because the puppet script is a short, tight script, audience members cannot pick it up in the middle and expect to understand what is going on. The noise outdoors or in a shopping mall makes it difficult for the performer to concentrate and for the audience to enjoy the show. Also, the audience should ideally be close to the puppet theater. When the audience views the play from a raised stage far away, much of the intimacy is lost, as are many of the visual and auditory nuances.

One of the less obvious lessons a young audience learns in viewing puppetry is proper audience behavior—how to be a good audience listener and participator. Puppetry is an experience like regular storytelling, which is built on a personal dramatic rapport with the puppeteer or storyteller. The young audience member has to realize that the storyteller or puppeteer doesn't come with a mute button, on-off switch, pause button, or volume control. Concentration is necessary. It doesn't take long, however, for audiences of all ages to fall under the magical spell of a puppet show. To get started, you will need to create the puppets and the stage. Then you are ready to choose the right script, to rehearse, and finally to perform!

Chapter 2

Creating the Puppets and Stage

*F*or any of the plays described in this book, you can use ready-made puppets or wooden stages. But to keep costs down and make your stage more portable, follow the tips below and create your own inexpensive puppets and a lightweight, easy-to-carry stage.

WHAT TYPES OF PUPPETS ARE EASIEST TO CREATE AND USE?

Although the quickest way to find suitable puppets may be to purchase them in stores or online, these ready-made puppets will often be quite expensive, especially if you are trying to amass a whole collection of puppets at one time. You might want to buy at first a few professionally produced puppets, like a bear, a wolf, or a rabbit, that you know you will use in several scripts. You may find, though, that even if you are willing to buy certain puppets, you cannot find all the animal or human puppet figures that you need. (By doing a Google search for the type of puppet you need, "shark puppet," for example, you can often locate a puppet source online.)

Although many types of puppets are possible to make (for example, puppets made from paper bags, paper stick puppets, felt puppets, wooden puppets, etc.), the longest-lasting and easiest types to use and store are the hand puppets made from stuffed animal toys and the hand puppets made using either a doll's head or a papier-mâché head attached to a glove body shape. Here are tips for creating these types of puppets.

Stuffed Toy Puppets

Stuffed toy puppets are the easiest and quickest puppets to make. You can readily find cheap, usable stuffed animals, cloth dolls, and other stuffed toys at dollar stores, flea markets, or garage sales if you don't have some in your home to use. (I recently found that many unusual animal stuffed toys can be found in pet stores!) I am an inveterate shopper as well as collector, and I'm always on the prowl for toys or other objects that can be converted into puppets. (I have even made hand puppets out of oven mitts—before the mitt became a talking puppet for a fast-food chain—and from fluffy slippers that had animal heads on them.)

Here's what to look for: keep in mind that you want a doll or toy that fits your whole hand comfortably. Beanie Baby–sized animals, though available at many sales, are too small to use as hand puppets. Hold up your hand to the back of the toy to test the size. Also, look for toys that have arms and legs that you can get your fingers into from the inside. (Sometimes the limbs are just stitched to the body from the outside, and you will have to take off the

FIGURE 2-1

limbs and reattach them after you poke holes for them in the body.) (Another tip: limit the use of puppets made from recognizable cartoon or television characters like Mickey Mouse, Big Bird, or Barney, for example. I have performed puppet shows with a Kermit figure as the frog character, and all I heard from behind the stage during most of the play were cries of "Kermit.")

Although the puppets made from stuffed toys will probably not have movable mouths, that really should not be a problem. If children are using their imaginations by imagining that the puppet is a certain animal, they can also easily imagine that the animal is talking without seeing the mouth actually move.

To convert a stuffed toy quickly into a puppet, slit the back open 4″ or 5″ and place your hand inside. If you cut open a back seam, reinforce the stitching at the ends of your slit to prevent the material from unraveling. If you make your cut horizontally, not on the seam, you will probably not have to reinforce your stitches. One or two fingers (second and third fingers) should fit in the head to support the head of the puppet. Your thumb could move one of the arms, while the fourth finger can move the other arm. The little finger can be folded under or can work with the fourth finger in moving an arm. Figure 2-1 shows two stuffed-toy puppets.

Remove enough stuffing to allow your hand to fit comfortably in the body, but leave enough in to give shape to the body (see figure 2-2).

FIGURE 2-2

Doll-Headed Puppets

You most likely will not be able to locate ready-made stuffed toys for some of your animal and human characters. In these cases you can create a custom-made puppet by gluing a doll's head onto a glove-shaped material body. (This same body pattern can be used for the body of a puppet with a papier-mâché head described below.) Follow the directions in figure 2-3 to construct the

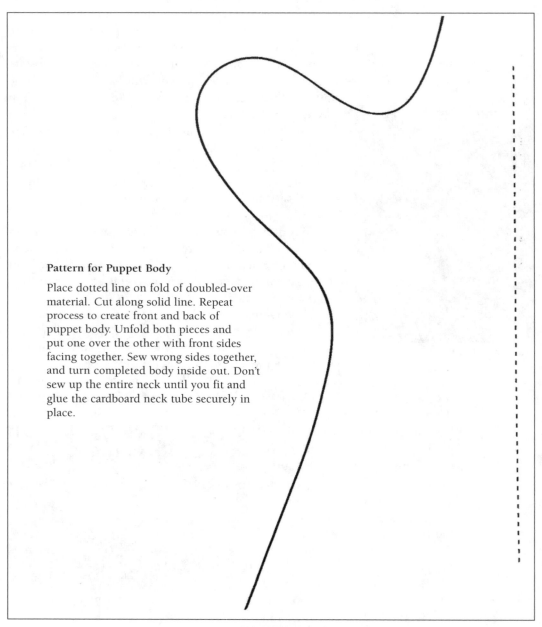

Pattern for Puppet Body

Place dotted line on fold of doubled-over material. Cut along solid line. Repeat process to create front and back of puppet body. Unfold both pieces and put one over the other with front sides facing together. Sew wrong sides together, and turn completed body inside out. Don't sew up the entire neck until you fit and glue the cardboard neck tube securely in place.

FIGURE 2-3

glove body. Remember to place the right side of the pattern on the fold of the doubled-over piece of material, so that the front and back are each one piece of material. You will need to cut two pieces: one for the back and one for the front of the puppet.

Most dolls' heads are not meant to be supported by your fingers. You may have to enlarge the hole in the doll's head so that one or two fingers can fit in comfortably. Many doll heads have a neck attached. If the head has a neck, you can glue the neck of the cloth body directly to the neck. If there is not a neck, you may need to fit a cardboard tube tightly in the head so that you can glue the cloth body onto the cardboard tube. Attach the head to the cloth body with Tacky Glue or other strong craft glue and reinforce with a rubber band until the glue is completely dry. Look for fabric remnants that will fit the character of your doll's head. If you want to adorn the glove body, you can use a scrap of material for a cape, hood, scarf, or shawl. Fine and careful stitching is not necessary since the stitching cannot be seen from a distance by the audience. If doll hands come with the doll head, and if you would rather use them than have cloth mitts for the puppet, you can cut

FIGURE 2-4

a small hole in the mitt ends of the glove body, insert the hands in the hole, and sew the hole shut tightly around the plastic doll hands (see figure 2-4).

Papier-Mâché-Headed Dolls

If you have the time and materials to create your own original glove puppets, one of the most durable types to try is made with a papier-mâché head glued on a material body. Don't expect the results to be as realistic with papier-mâché as you would get from stuffed toys or dolls' heads, but there is a charm and character to these original puppet creations. These puppet heads are practically indestructible too. Although you can fashion these heads with regular papier-mâché made from torn newspaper and glue, you can also save time and mess by using a premade papier-mâché called Celluclay or Celluclay II. Follow the simple if somewhat messy directions for mixing up a batch of Celluclay. (Be prepared for a lot of paper dust as you mix the water in. I usually add a couple of squirts of Elmer's glue into the mix, just to give it a little more stickiness and strength. You want the mixture to be wet enough to be easy to work with, but not too wet and runny.)

Begin with a Styrofoam oval that is approximately the size you want for the head of your puppet. For most puppets you will want an oval egg of

Styrofoam that is about 3″ to 4″. An oval shape is best used for a human figure, while a ball shape works well for an animal's head. Force a cardboard tube (about the diameter of a tube from a roll of toilet paper) an inch or so into the Styrofoam egg. The tube will act as a neck for the puppet and a place for your two fingers to support the head (see figure 2-5). Choose the sturdiest tubes you can find. Once the tube is in place, work a bit of the Styrofoam away from the inside

FIGURE 2-5

with the tips of a scissors so that your fingers can fit in comfortably to support the head. Holding onto the cardboard tube, spread a layer of Celluclay over the Styrofoam egg or ball. Extend the Celluclay an inch or so onto the tube so that the Styrofoam will attach well to the tube. You can insert a rod, such as a pencil, into the Styrofoam head, and then push the other end of the rod into a block of Styrofoam, a large sponge, or a bottle until the clay has set on the head (see figure 2-6). This allows the head to dry evenly. After the first layer dries, you can add some more Celluclay, if you wish to add more features. Be sure to allow sufficient drying time between layers. Let the heads dry for at least two days, longer if the Celluclay is heavily applied. You can usually see when the papier-mâché is dry, because the dry part will be lighter than

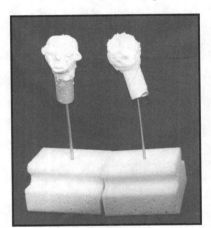

FIGURE 2-6

sections that are still moist. You can mold simple features into the Celluclay, like eyebrows, nose, and mouth, but be careful not to pile too much Celluclay on the head. Remember that you will have to support the head with two fingers, so you do not want the head to be too heavy and uncomfortable to support, and most of the detailed features can be added with paint.

Tip: if you are creating a large figure like a giant, it is better to start with a larger Styrofoam head rather than to layer on the clay too thickly. After the Celluclay is well dried, in two or three days, you can paint on features (see figures 2-7 and 2-8).

After painting, varnish the heads to preserve the painted features. Finally, make a glove body of appropriate material and glue the neck of the material body to the cardboard-tube neck. Thick craft glue (like Tacky Glue) works best for this. Trim back the tube to a comfortable length for your fingers, leaving about 1 ½″ of neck. Although this method of puppet-head construction does take some time and effort to accomplish, you can produce any kind of human or animal puppet that you might need. This method is particularly useful for making characters for which doll heads or stuffed toys are hard to find—especially human figures like men, boys, and older women. With

FIGURE 2-7

FIGURE 2-8

papier-mâché you can make distinctive and original puppets. Because the creation of these papier-mâché heads is a craft or art project, you might try this in the library or the classroom as a group art project. I have used this method with a group of adults and children to create puppets for our library programs.

WHAT TYPE OF STAGE IS EASIEST TO USE?

You can, of course, use a traditional wooden puppet stage to perform any of the one-person shows in this book or any of the scripts you might write yourself. If you use this type of stage, you sit on a chair or stool in back of the stage and perform by extending your arms up with the puppets attached. I think, however, it is much easier on your arms to use a different type of inexpensive, portable stage that you can quickly create yourself (see figure 2-9).

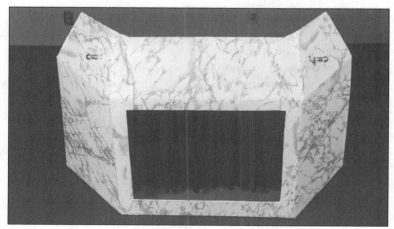

FIGURE 2-9

Ideally, the stage should fit easily in your car, require minimal time for setup, and be light enough for you to carry by yourself. I have fashioned for my own shows two sizes of puppet stages. Both are made from cardboard cartons and covered with contact paper to make them more durable and attractive. Both are meant to be used on a tabletop. (The size of the carton is not critical, as long as you can comfortably fit inside and be hidden from view of the audience when you are seated.) The smaller stage I made is constructed from a carton that was 21″ wide, 14″ deep, and 16″ tall. The larger stage was made from a carton that was 42″ wide, 7″ deep, and 18″ high. Both sizes work well, but the larger stage is easier to use with longer scripts. Pick a carton that is tall enough for you to be hidden (when you are seated) from the audience behind the stage when the carton is placed on a tabletop. By folding the top flaps of the carton upward to form a roof (as shown in figure 2-9), you gain several inches of height. For the smaller carton, for example, I gained about 7 ½″ with the top flaps raised, and for the larger stage, I gained about 7″. Your stage will sit on a table covered by a sheet or tablecloth to hide your legs and feet. (I once forgot the table covering for an assembly performance on a raised stage and was told too late that the audience could see my legs and feet all during the performance. Besides my being embarrassed, the puppetry illusion was ruined.)

To create the stage, you need a large carton, an X-Acto cutting knife, a ruler or yardstick, a few brass fastening brads, a pencil, a piece of material for the curtain, a lightweight but extendable drapery pole, a needle and thread to sew up the curtain, and Velcro to attach the scripts.

First place your carton with the widest side of the carton resting on a table. Designate the front of the carton as the side you will use to cut the stage opening. Measure and mark one-half of the back of the carton and cut all the way down the back. These two half back flaps, along with the sides of the carton depth, will create the area for you to be enclosed in behind the stage.

Lift the top flaps of the carton upward and fashion the roof by fastening the cardboard pieces on each side with a brad, creating a roof shape (figure 2-10 provides step-by-step stage-building directions).

Once the stage itself is built, pencil in and then cut out an area for your proscenium with the X-Acto knife, leaving a border of 4″ or so of cardboard on each side so that your stage will be stable. Punch a hole on each side at the top of the theater (5″ or so from the top) for a metal pole to fit through.

Make a simple curtain for the theater by sewing a pocket in the material for the pole to fit through. Hem the curtain fabric. Make sure that your curtain is long enough to extend to the bottom of the stage floor, not just to the bottom of the stage opening. A dark, plain curtain works best, fashioned from a medium- to heavyweight fabric remnant. (Don't use too flimsy a material or it will not support the weight of your scripts.) When you hang your curtain on a lightweight, extendable drapery pole and put the pole in place, your construction is complete. Your pole also acts as a good handle for transporting the stage to your car.

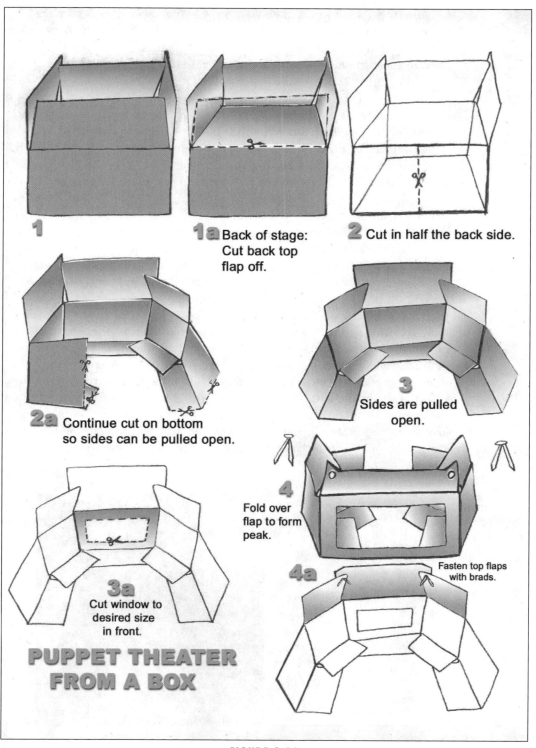

1

1a Back of stage:
Cut back top
flap off.

2 Cut in half the back side.

2a Continue cut on bottom
so sides can be pulled open.

3 Sides are pulled
open.

4 Fold over
flap to form
peak.

3a Cut window to
desired size
in front.

**PUPPET THEATER
FROM A BOX**

4a Fasten top flaps
with brads.

FIGURE 2-10

You might wish to decorate your stage by covering the entire stage with weatherproof contact paper. Your scripts can be attached to the back of the curtain so that you can reach under the curtain and operate your puppets in front of the curtain. This allows you to read your scripts at eye level as you move the puppets.

Your curtain should be wide enough to accommodate four or more 8 ½″ by 11″ script pages, side by side. That should work for most of the play scripts in this book. If the script you choose is longer than that, you can either reduce the print on the script pages in a copier, or you can place the script sheets back to back so that they can easily be reversed. If your stage accommodates five sheets side by side, for example, place script page 6 on the back of page 1, page 7 on the back of page 2, and so forth. Put a piece of Velcro on the top of each side of the pages so that you can quickly switch sides of the scripts during a short intermission.

When the stage is set up on a tabletop, you can usually extend the wings of the carton outward to get more curtain room for scripts (see figure 2-11).

For the first several years of doing puppet shows with my portable stage, I relied on pinning the scripts directly onto the curtain. You can either pin the scripts directly on the curtain, or pin plastic protector sheets on the curtain, and then slip the pages for the scripts in and out of these folders. One of the limitations with this pinning method is that you will be delayed between shows when you have to change script pages. I have recently had more success using Velcro rather than straight pins. Run a strip of Velcro the width of the whole curtain a few inches from the top of the stage curtain on the inside. Then laminate or use clear Contac paper on your script pages to give them substance (this way they will not curl up as much), and attach a small strip of Velcro to the back of each of the pages. Now you can take the

FIGURE 2-11

scripts off and place new ones on in a matter of seconds. Be sure that your scripts are attached securely to the curtain and are high enough on the curtain so that they will not be jostled every time you move your puppets from underneath.

Because you are going to be talking into a curtain, and also because changing voices takes a lot of vocal energy, it is a good idea to have a small wireless microphone and speaker you can use for your scripts. I travel with a small portable microphone and speaker that I purchased at an electronic store in case the school or library's microphone and speaker don't work. You may be tempted to skip a microphone and rely on the volume of your own voice, but remember that nothing is more frustrating for the audience than not to be able to hear well what the puppet characters are saying. You will find that without a microphone, even in a small classroom, you may be straining your voice after a few shows.

Also, be sure to have a straight chair available for you to sit on in back of your stage as well as a long table wide enough to support your opened table-top stage. With the puppets and stage completed, you're ready to move on to the puppet scripts themselves. In the next chapter, I provide some performance tips and warm-up exercises.

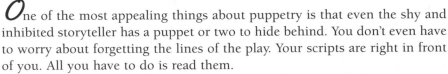

Chapter 3

Showtime: Preparing and Delivering the Performance

*O*ne of the most appealing things about puppetry is that even the shy and inhibited storyteller has a puppet or two to hide behind. You don't even have to worry about forgetting the lines of the play. Your scripts are right in front of you. All you have to do is read them.

However, don't be fooled into thinking that just because you have the script in front of you, you don't need to practice before a performance. You should be very familiar with the story lines and with the scripts, because without sufficient practice, things are much more likely to go wrong. I have forgotten to have a puppet character enter or exit at the correct time, had scripts fall off the curtain as I was performing (that was when I was pinning the scripts), had script pages disappear when I was midway through the play, had puppet heads come off in midsentence, and had young children grab at the performing puppet actors. (More on how to handle those "disasters" later.) With practice and a certain comfort level with the scripts, you'll be free to ad-lib some lines should such mishaps occur. Practice and planning are key to reaching a comfort level with your scripts. In this chapter, I show you some tips for warming up, planning the performance, and performing the show.

FIRST, THE WARM-UP

One great technique for practicing some of the voices you'll be creating or preparing for a performance is to try some warm-up exercises borrowed from actors. Try a warm-up exercise like the one below to experiment with creating various voices. You can use this exercise by yourself, or you can lead your class or group of children by having them repeat your initial phrase. Experiment by reading the lines in different voices—the voice of a baby, a squirrel, a prince, a wolf, a troll, or a lamb, for example. In character say the following rhythmic lines (if you are using this as a class warm-up exercise, you can say the line first and have the class repeat the line in the appropriate voice).

> Down on the bottom
> Down on the bottom
> Down on the bottom, on the bottom of the sea.
> Down on the bottom, on the bottom of the sea.
> Swimming around,
> Swimming around,
> Lurking around,
> Lurking around,
> Watch your toes.
> Watch your toes.
> Don't look now.
> Don't look now.
> It's got you!
> It's got you!

When you are properly warmed up, you are ready to practice reading through the script. First read the whole script through several times without using any voice changes. Just become familiar with the lines. Then you can begin to create different voices. Even though there are only two or three characters in the whole play, you alone will be performing all the voices, and you will want each voice to be distinctive in some way. Develop one voice at a time, and with that puppet on your hand, read the lines of that one character. Narrator lines can be read in your own normal voice and should be read as clearly as possible, since the narrator provides many of the important plot details.

Experiment with voice changes—reading lines in a lower pitch for a male character and a higher voice for a female character. The same is true for animal characters. A squirrel's voice, for example, should be high-pitched and chattery, while a lion's voice should be deep, rich, and regal. After you have practiced the lines of the script with one character, start creating the other voices in the same way. Finally, put all of your voices together as you read the entire script through. Give yourself time between character changes to switch voices. As you read through the characters' parts, remember: you can be as expressive as you want to be. In fact, the more exaggerated the expression, the better. Although you want to be expressive, however, be sure not to strain your voice with any one character's voice. (This is why a microphone is so essential in the one-person performance too, so that you can avoid straining your voice and still be loud enough to be understood. You are speaking into a curtain, after all, and this will muffle your voice if you are not using a microphone.) Remember, timing is important. Don't rush through the lines of the play. During the performance, you'll want to give your audience time to absorb the words in each line of the scripts. After all, you are very familiar with the lines by now, but your audience is hearing the lines for the first time. Because it is difficult to change back and forth quickly using different voices, read over the whole script many times until you are comfortable both with the lines and with the voice changes.

Another important area to practice before showtime is the manipulation of the puppets themselves. After you have read through the whole script with different voices, read through the scripts with the puppets on your hands using the portable stage. Practice all the appropriate gestures, movements, entrances, and exits. Given the configuration of the stage, you will not be able to see what your puppets are doing in front of your curtain, so practice keeping your movements clear and simple. When one puppet is talking, move only that puppet, letting it gesture. Keep the other puppet still as it "listens." That way the audience can clearly identify who is speaking. And it also will make it easier on you. (Once during a show, I had two characters answering back and forth, and I forgot which puppet was on which hand. From that point on, I clearly marked on the top of the script which puppet was on which hand.)

At the top of your scripts, print which puppet is to be used on the right hand and which is to be manipulated by the left. When you practice, use the same puppet on the same hand you will use in the performance. If you are right-handed, use your right hand for the more "active" puppet—the one who moves around and exits and enters more than the other puppet. If you are left-handed, the more active puppet should be on your left hand.

Once you have performed a number of shows, you will probably have chosen your favorite scripts to perform. The shows will get better, the voices more expressive, and the plays easier for you to perform the more often you perform them. When you are comfortable with the lines of the scripts, the voices you have created, and the physical manipulations of the puppets, you are ready to perform.

PREPARING YOUR PROPS AND PUPPETS

After you have performed a few scripts, you'll see why a one-person puppeteer doesn't use many—or even any—props. It takes a lot of practice to handle even simple props with your puppet characters. Sometimes a show requires a prop, like a letter or a stick. These types of props can be pinned, taped, or attached with Velcro to the puppet's hand so that you don't have to make the puppet carry a prop onstage or pick up an item while it is performing. For some essential props, like the bridge that the troll lives under, place the prop onstage before the play begins.

Puppet-show props can be made from scraps of materials or even disposable packing materials. Styrofoam packing materials often are precut to some strange shapes that can be adapted to a needed prop. Styrofoam pieces can also be torn to resemble rocks or painted with acrylic paints.

You'll want to practice to get comfortable with your puppets as well. After you perform a few shows, you will see why puppets with light heads are the easiest to manipulate. Be sure that your fingers comfortably support the puppet heads during the shows, or your puppet heads may sag as your wrists and arms get tired. Also, be sure that your puppets are securely on your hands before putting them onstage. You may be a little rushed between shows, but take the extra second or two to make sure that your hand is comfortably in your puppet character so that the puppet can stand and perform with good posture. After you complete a puppet script, it is wise to say, "The End," and have the two puppet characters take a bow. You are dealing with a young audience, after all, and you want to be sure that they realize that script is over.

PUTTING IT ALL TOGETHER

After you have assembled your puppets, your scripts, and your stage, and after you have warmed up your voice with an exercise and practiced your scripts, the next step will be planning your program.

What kind of program should you plan? Puppetry can be used in many ways in a storytelling program and of course needs to be geared to the age of the audience members and their attention span. My recommendation for a regular library or classroom puppet performance is a show that consists of either three or four performed scripts with intermissions between the plays. These short breaks give the audience a chance to relax and even participate in the performance. They also give you a chance to change dramatic gears and voices for the next show—changing scripts, getting the puppets ready, and so forth. (See the boxed text for tips on using puppetry during story times.)

I have found that thirty or forty minutes is a good length for your puppet program, even if you are dealing with a middle-school audience. I always take the advice my father gave me in performing: to leave your audience wanting more, not wishing for an end to the show.

It's up to you which scripts you choose for a performance. I like to mix types and lengths of scripts. You may, for example, begin with a short humorous play to get the audience's attention, and then alternate with a longer, more serious play. You can plan all the scripts around one theme or mix scripts together that are appropriate for a season or holiday.

After one script is over, have all your puppets and scripts ready for a quick change for the next show. I think that Velcro works best for changing scripts quickly between shows. I have the puppets and props for each show bagged separately and scripts all together organized in a plastic file.

When you feel that you or the audience needs a break from the shows, try alternating a script with a short poem performed either by a puppet from behind the stage or by a larger puppet with which you can come out in front of the audience. You might also use a flannel-board story between puppet plays, a simple origami animal you can make with the audience, or a visual story that you can draw as you talk.

USING PUPPETS DURING STORY TIMES

Librarians and teachers can use puppetry in different ways for story times with children. Instead of reading a book yourself, use a puppet to read the entire book, or act out part of the text with one or two puppets. Instead of taking a puppet or puppets on and off your hands during the story while you are trying to turn the pages of the book, you can try using a large sponge as a base for mounting a puppet body on a table. I use the largest sponges I can find as a base (about 2" thick and perhaps 4" by 6"), and a long knitting needle placed in the sponge base supports the puppet and holds it upright (see figure). As you read the book to the group, showing the pictures as you read, you can merely point to the puppet or move it about slightly.

You might prefer to use a puppet stage during a story time, but instead of performing several puppet scripts, you might wish to perform a single short puppet script. Your small, portable tabletop stage is versatile to use for this single script as well as for longer programs.

You can also use riddles appropriate to the season or to the theme of the show. You can either have the puppeteer or a large puppet ask the riddles. For example, for a spring show, use some frog riddles after performing a play about a frog. You might come to the front of the audience with a large frog on your arm that can "help" you deliver the riddles. (You can easily make these larger puppets from large stuffed animals in the same way that you make the smaller stage puppets.) You can pretend to have a large puppet character whisper the riddle or the answer in your ear, for example, and you don't have to use ventriloquism. For an Easter show, use a large rabbit for asking bunny riddles. For Thanksgiving, use some turkey riddles or jokes. Before or after performing a script with dinosaurs as characters, you can use a large dinosaur in front of the stage to ask some dinosaur riddles. (See suggestions for riddle books in appendix C.) If you haunt the stores immediately after a holiday, you can often purchase large stuffed animals suitable to be made into puppets at a greatly reduced price.

For variety, songs are always good to include between show scripts. Perhaps the best songs to use are participation songs, because they give the audience a chance to move around a bit before the next show. If you want to add a little variety, try writing and singing song parodies to familiar melodies that the children already know. Instead of singing the original words to the song "B-I-N-G-O," for example, try singing, "There was a teacher [or parent] had a child who was an avid [or summer] reader. R-E-A-D-E-R," and so forth. (See the list of recommended songs and the parodies to use in appendix A.)

If you're going to sing during breaks between scripts, it's probably best to use songs that the audience already knows. You do not have time to teach songs to the audience during a short intermission. If you are in a library, parents in the audience will mostly likely know the songs and can help lead the children. Songs like "B-I-N-G-O" or "Put Your Finger in the Air" are examples of good participation songs that can get the audience actively involved. As with the riddle exercise, you can also use a large puppet to help lead the singing. A large dog puppet, for example, would be a good leader for the song "B-I-N-G-O," or a large rabbit or frog figure would be a good leader for a spring puppet-show song.

If you know a musical instrument like the guitar or piano, it is fun to play the melodies for the audience first or to accompany the song. Playing an instrument like the Autoharp, the Melodica, a small accordion, or a small keyboard also can add to the singing and audience participation.

BECOMING PARTNERS WITH YOUR PUPPETS

We've already talked about using large puppets to help tell riddles or lead songs. I have also found it helpful to use a large puppet character as a kind of librarian's or teacher's helper, storytelling mascot, or class mascot. You might wish to have a large puppet figure on your arm act as the narrator or emcee several times during the whole performance. (See appendix B for an example of how a large dinosaur puppet can be used as an emcee for a Christmas show.) As an emcee or storytelling mascot, a large puppet can be used as an attention getter and even as a disciplinarian to bring the audience to attention. If some students are talking, or if some are not ready to pay attention to a story time, for example, a puppet character can make a comment of correction or irritation or simply call the group to order. The puppet can also indicate to you in your ear that he is too scared to come out and speak while the other talking is going on. This can save the librarian or the teacher from having to correct the inattentive children directly.

As discussed earlier, I also use some big puppets made from large stuffed toys to entertain the audience between short plays. It is remarkable how the attention of the children is on the puppet and its gestures, not on you as the speaking person. Also, be prepared to react freely with the puppet, as if you are willing to suspend your disbelief along with the audience. If you expect children to believe in the reality of the puppet, you must too—even if at first you may feel a little foolish in doing so.

WHAT HAPPENS IF YOU MAKE A MISTAKE?

Misplacing script pages, having puppet heads pop off, losing your place: you can get extremely nervous and upset by these possible mishaps, or you can take them in stride and make the mishap a humorous or even planned part of the show. When I have flubbed a script line, I try to work the mistake into the script. If a character loses his head, for example, you might have the narrator comment that that puppet got himself so worked up he lost his head. Then you can ask the audience members if they would be willing to wait until he got himself all together again. Ask if they would encourage the puppet to come out again, because he was embarrassed. Usually involving the audience will make them more interested, and they might even cheer the puppet's return onstage. If you cannot cover the mistake easily, you can always apologize afterward for your puppet actors, saying that they were extremely nervous or tired and that is what caused them to make mistakes. You can always blame the puppets. Thankfully, they are not able to answer back.

BREAK A LEG!

There are many wonderful books on the subject of puppetry that you can read before you perform; some are even specifically on the use of one-person puppetry (see appendix E for a bibliography of recommended books on puppetry). Although the advice I have given and the directions I have explained here may not always agree with the advice and directions in other puppet books, my techniques do work. I have tried in this book to suggest some tips and tricks for making one-person puppetry less complicated and easier for librarians, teachers, parents, grandparents, and students to attempt. You have directions for everything you need here to get you started in performing one-person puppet shows for children in the library, in the classroom, or at home. The scripts that follow are ready for you to use. You can just copy them, laminate them, and attach them with Velcro to your theater curtain. Of course you can also just use these scripts as models for writing your own puppet plays.

One-person puppetry gives you a wonderful chance to let your imagination run free in a number of directions. Don't be overwhelmed or intimidated! I hope this book stimulates your creative juices as well as those of your audiences. Just let yourself enter into the pleasurable fantasy that puppetry can provide! I realize that I am an amateur puppeteer, but remember that the word *amateur* comes from the Latin word *amare,* meaning "to love." Hopefully, after you have a few one-person puppet performances behind you, you too will become an "amateur" puppeteer.

Part Two

PUPPET SCRIPTS

Aladdin's Magic Lamp

(a retelling of the tale of Aladdin)

Puppets needed:
   Aladdin
   Genie

Props:
   magic lamp (optional)
   bags of money

NARRATOR: *(Aladdin enters)* Once upon a time in the fabled city of Samarkand in the distant province of Turkestan, a young man called Aladdin lived with his mother. Now, Aladdin was a poor man, but he was also rather lazy, and his mother had to nag him about finding work so that they would have money to buy food to eat. When Aladdin was in the market-place one day, a stranger offered him a well-paying job if he would do his bidding without raising any questions. Aladdin accepted the job not knowing that the stranger was really an evil magician who was searching for secret treasure in a nearby cave. He led Aladdin to the entrance of the cave and told him to enter the cave and search for a lamp that he had left there earlier. Aladdin saw many boxes of jewels as he searched for the lamp, and he secretly stuffed some jewels in his pockets. When he found the lamp, he headed back to the man, but when the magician demanded the lamp, Aladdin refused to hand it over to him. For disobeying his order, the magician used his magic to close off the cave with Aladdin in it. Aladdin remained in the cave for two days and was about to give up on escaping when he accidentally rubbed the side of the lamp. Suddenly a genie appeared beside him.

GENIE: *(Enters)* Who are you and what do you want from me? I am the Genie of the lamp, and while you possess this magic lamp, your wish is my command.

ALADDIN: Oh, Genie, I am only a poor man named Aladdin, and I have only one wish—to get out of this cave. Can you get me out of here?

GENIE: That I can do. Where do you want me to take you, Master?

ALADDIN: Home, please.

GENIE: Done. *(Exits)*

NARRATOR:	And instantly Aladdin found himself in his own home with his mother. *(Move Aladdin to the other side of the stage)* His mother complained to Aladdin that there was no food or money in the house, since he had left home. When his mother wasn't looking, Aladdin rubbed the lamp again.
GENIE:	*(Enters)* I am here, Master. What is your wish now?
ALADDIN:	I wish to have some food for our table and some money for other needs.
GENIE:	As you desire, Sire. *(Exits and reenters with bags)*
ALADDIN:	Thank you, Genie. This will do nicely.

(Genie exits)

NARRATOR:	And Genie left behind trays of food and bags of money—enough for quite some time. After a while, however, Aladdin's mother began to nag her son about getting a job so he could find a wife and start a family one day. That started Aladdin thinking.
ALADDIN:	I think I'll make another wish. I'll rub the lamp again. *(Rubs lamp)*
GENIE:	*(Enters)* Yes, Master. What is your wish today?
ALADDIN:	I would like to have a lovely woman as my wife as well as all the riches we would need for a good life together.
GENIE:	Certainly, Master. What type of wife do you desire, Master?
ALADDIN:	If I can have any woman I want, I choose the lovely daughter of the sultan as my future wife.
GENIE:	Well, that certainly is aiming high. It is difficult but not impossible. The sultan is a greedy man. What you must do first is to offer him some very expensive gifts so that he will recognize your name. I will have a box of fine jewels sent to the sultan in your name. *(Exits)*
NARRATOR:	The sultan accepted the gifts but made it known in a note that he required forty baskets filled with precious stones before he would consider Aladdin as a suitor for his daughter's hand in marriage. Once again, Aladdin rubbed the lamp.
ALADDIN:	*(Rubs lamp)* Here goes.
GENIE:	*(Enters)* Yes, Master?
ALADDIN:	I have a note back from the sultan that I must now provide him with forty baskets of jewels before I can marry the princess.
GENIE:	I will see to it. *(Exits)*
NARRATOR:	And Genie arranged for the delivery of the jewels to the sultan. When the sultan received the jewels, he was convinced that Aladdin was very, very rich, so he gave him permission to marry his daughter.

GENIE: *(Enters)* It is done as you wish, Master. Now I must prepare you to meet the sultan at the palace. I will clothe you in the finest golden robes and conjure up a fine horse for you to ride to the palace. When I am through, no one would ever recognize you as the son of a tailor. I will also build you and your bride a fine home—as fine a home as the sultan's palace—maybe finer. *(Both exit)*

NARRATOR: All went well for Aladdin and his beautiful bride, and they wanted for nothing. One day, however, the evil magician heard stories about a rich man called Aladdin and his bride, and he realized that Aladdin must have escaped from the cave with the magic lamp. The magician was determined to have the lamp for himself and went to Aladdin's home disguised as a beggar woman when Aladdin was out hunting. He asked Aladdin's wife if she could spare any of the old lamps in the house that they no longer needed. Not knowing that this was a magic lamp, the princess gave the magician Aladdin's lamp. When Aladdin returned home and learned of this, he was very upset.

ALADDIN: *(Enters)* What will I do now? I must find the lamp and my Genie. I will ask my wife to invite the magician to our home so that I may steal the lamp back. I will have her put a sleeping potion in his tea. *(Exits)*

NARRATOR: And so Aladdin asked his wife to invite the magician to tea. The princess put a potion in the drink of the magician, and Aladdin was able to steal back Aladdin's lamp.

ALADDIN: *(Enters)* I will rub the lamp once again. *(Rubs lamp)*

GENIE: *(Enters)* Yes, Master? How may I help you?

ALADDIN: *First,* please make that evil magician disappear, and then I wish you to make our wedded life as happy as it was before the magician came.

GENIE: It will be as you wish. In fact, I will give you one gift without your asking for it.

NARRATOR: What was that one gift, you ask? Genie's gift was that Aladdin and his princess would live happily together for many years, raising a large, happy, virtuous family. Aladdin never again lost track of the wonderful lamp. It wasn't that Aladdin needed any more wishes, though. These days Genie often comes out of the lamp, but not just to work; now he comes out to attend family parties as an honored guest. You see, now Aladdin and his princess are able to make their own good fortune together, all by themselves.

The End

A Bit of Magic

(a retelling of "The Magic Pot")

Puppets needed:
Widow
Child

Prop:
magic pot (optional)

NARRATOR: Once upon a time there was a poor widow who lived with her daughter in a small village. Life was always hard for the two of them, but when the widow lost her job as a cook for a wealthy family, there was little in the pantry for her and her child to eat. One day she walked deep into the woods and came upon a well-tended cottage. The old woman who answered the door felt sorry for the young widow after she heard her story, so she gave her a special present—a magic pot. This pot would always cook up a good, hearty meal: a flavorful porridge. Whenever the widow needed a meal for herself and her child, the pot would provide it. The old woman warned the widow about two things she would have to remember about the pot: she could share the food but never reveal the fact that the pot was magic to anyone but her daughter. Also, she had to use the proper words to start and to end the pot's work. To get the pot to cook up a meal, she had to say, "Please start, pot." For the pot to stop cooking, she had to say, "Thank you, pot. Stop now, please." The widow thanked the old woman and hurried home to feed her hungry daughter a good breakfast.

(Widow and daughter enter)

WIDOW: Oh, look, Daughter, what your mother has gotten from a kind old woman—a magic pot that will keep us fed every day. No more going hungry to school or hungry to bed at night.

CHILD: That's wonderful, Mother. Let's try it at once. What are the magic words we have to say to start it up?

WIDOW: Before we start, we must remember to do two things. First we must not tell anyone else about our wonderful pot. Next, to start the pot, we must say the words "Please start, pot." To end the cooking, we must say, "Thank you, pot. Stop now, please." Let's start it up now. Please start, pot. Please start our breakfast, magic pot.

NARRATOR: And the pot started bubbling away in the kitchen.
(Say "Blub, blub. Blub, blub")

WIDOW:	This looks and smells like wonderful porridge. Try it, dear.
CHILD:	Oh, yes, Mother. This is the best porridge I have ever tasted. It's even got cream and sugar mixed in.
WIDOW:	Now we must say, "Thank you, pot. Stop now, please."

(Mother and daughter exit)

NARRATOR:	The pot suddenly stopped bubbling, and the leftover porridge in the pot disappeared, leaving the pot completely clean and ready for the next meal. In the next few months, the widow's life was a lot easier, since she took in sewing and didn't have to worry about feeding herself and her daughter. She now even had enough food to serve friends of hers and her daughter's when they came to visit. As the months went on, however, the widow grew a bit tired of porridge. She wondered if she could exchange this pot for another magic pot that would serve different meals, so she went to the old woman's cottage to ask. The old woman was still sorry for the young widow, so she took the first pot back and gave her a second magic pot. Again she warned the widow that she would have to say the correct magic words to end the cooking: "Thank you, pot. Stop now, please." If ever the pot were to boil over without the widow saying those words, the pot would lose its magic. For a while again the widow and her daughter were very content with the second pot, but one day at breakfast they talked about it.
WIDOW:	*(Enters with daughter)* Please start, pot.
NARRATOR:	The second pot heated away on its own and cooked up delicious omelets and sausage.
WIDOW:	These are tasty eggs and sausage, but I'm getting sick of eggs all the time. Sometimes I wish we had our first porridge pot back.
CHILD:	Yes, Mother, that porridge was always flavored so well. You didn't even need to add milk or sugar.
NARRATOR:	While they were talking, they didn't notice that the pot was boiling over. Finally they smelled the food coming from the kitchen.
WIDOW:	*(Sniffs)* Oh, no, the second pot has boiled over. *(Screams)* Stop, right now, pot. Stop, I said!
NARRATOR:	But the pot continued to produce more and more eggs and sausage, filling up the whole kitchen and moving through the house. Finally the daughter remembered the magic words.
CHILD:	Thank you, pot. Stop now, please.
NARRATOR:	Suddenly the flow of food ceased. This time, however, the remaining eggs and sausage were left, filling the whole kitchen and dining room.

WIDOW: Let's put away all the food that we can save in the refrigerator. Then we can ask all our neighbors in to eat the rest of all this food. It's a shame to waste all this wonderful food and let it spoil. We can even bring some of the food to the old woman in the cottage in the woods. I'll bet she would like a visitor and would like to meet you too, dear.

NARRATOR: And all the neighbors came over for breakfast for the next week—eating through the kitchen and dining room. After that, the widow and her daughter never went hungry again, but it was not the magic pot that fed them. No, the magic was gone from the pot, as the old woman had said. The new magic came from the fact that the widow and her daughter had shared their food with their neighbors. Now, whenever the widow and her daughter had little food left to eat, the neighbors brought over a pot of porridge or of stew.

WIDOW: It doesn't taste exactly like the porridge we had before, but it's good, isn't it, dear?

CHILD: You know, Mother, I will never complain about food again. And another thing, I'll never forget those magic words—*please* and *thank you.*

NARRATOR: Oh, by the way, the old woman gave the widow one more bit of magic after the second magic pot boiled over—her magic sewing needle. Quite a help for a young widow making her living now by sewing beautiful clothes!

The End

The Fisherman's Three Wishes

(a retelling of "The Fisherman and His Wife")

Puppets needed:

Fish

Fisherman

Props:

NARRATOR: Once upon a time there was a poor fisherman who went out each day to catch fish but never seemed to have much luck with either catching fish or making money. One day he caught a colorful fish in his net—a fish that was different from any fish he had ever caught. This fish could talk.

(Fish and Fisherman enter)

FISH: Please, Fisherman, throw me back in the water. I am really an enchanted fish with magical powers. If you put me back in the water, I promise to grant you one wish. Take a long time to consider well what that wish might be. Be sure you really want what you wish for.

FISHERMAN: OK, Fish, I will spare your life. I can tell you my wish without needing to take my time to consider it further. I know what I want. I want an exciting life and the money that goes along with that. I want to be very rich. I have been poor all my life. I know money will make me happy.

FISH: If you are sure that wealth is what you want, I will help you get that wish.

FISHERMAN: It is what I want. I would like to be rich right away.

FISH: Go home and you will find your fortune is waiting for you there.

(Both exit)

NARRATOR: And when the fisherman went to his old hut he discovered that in place of the hut was a magnificent mansion. Inside the mansion were ten bags of gold on the elegant dining room table. He was truly a wealthy man. For a few months, the fisherman was delighted with his new fortune. After a short while, though, he started to realize that with his new wealth there were many more expenses and worries: people were constantly begging him for money, and he had to guard his stacks of coins from thieves. He no longer had any time for fun. He decided that he needed a wife to share all this money and all this extra work of caring for the money. He went back to the spot in the sea where he had thrown back the magical fish.

FISHERMAN:	*(Enters)*
	Fish, oh, Fish of the sea,
	Remember the favor that you owe to me.
	I spared your life and lost a fish.
	Please grant me now a second wish.

NARRATOR: Soon the fish heard the fisherman's plea and appeared.

FISH: *(Enters)* Oh, it is you, Fisherman? Are you not now a wealthy man as I promised you would be? What more do you want from me? Are you not happy with the great wealth I gave to you? Are you seeking more money from me?

FISHERMAN: No, Fish, I do not wish more money. Although I am glad to have all the money, I have found that having wealth brings with it more responsibilities and more work than I had imagined. I need a wife to share this money with. But I do not want just any wife. I would like to marry the most beautiful woman in the village. Can you arrange that for me? I won't ask you for anything again.

FISH: Go home and she will be there waiting for you. But are you sure that you really want this second wish? Do you not know that beauty isn't everything in a wife?

FISHERMAN: I have thought of what would make me happy, and I know that having a very beautiful wife would be my best wish. Please be generous and grant me this second request.

(Fish and Fisherman exit)

NARRATOR: So the fisherman went home, and waiting for him in his mansion was the most beautiful woman he had ever seen. For a short time he was happy with his lovely wife, but it didn't take him long to realize that his new wife was more concerned with spending his money than with him. She spent her days buying expensive dresses and planning big parties. Lately his wife had been complaining that she wanted a much nicer home to live in and finer furnishings. The fisherman decided to take a chance and ask the fish for a third wish—an even bigger and more expensive mansion to live in.

FISHERMAN:	*(Enters)*
	Fish, oh, Fish of the sea,
	Remember the favor that you owe to me.
	I spared your life and lost a fish.
	Please grant me now a third wish.

FISH: *(Enters)* I am here, Fisherman. What now? First I grant you great wealth and then the most beautiful woman for your wife, and you still want more? When will you be satisfied?

FISHERMAN: My new wife would like a larger home to live in where we can entertain in grand style.

FISH: I warned you, Fisherman, to ask for just one thing. I was generous and granted you two wishes. Now you have made me mad with your greediness. Since you saved my life and I promised you one wish, I will leave you with one of your wishes, and one only. You may keep your beautiful wife, but the wealth I gave you will disappear as quickly as it came to you. Go home. I will not answer your call again.

(Both exit)

NARRATOR: And when the fisherman returned home, his beautiful wife was waiting for him in his old hut. She began to scream at him for losing the fine mansion, all her expensive clothes, and all the furnishings. Do you know what the fisherman did? No, he couldn't go back and ask the fish for any more help. He ran to his fishing boat and cast off to work. At least when he was fishing he didn't have to listen to his wife complain.

FISHERMAN: *(Enters)* If ever I catch another magical fish, I will be much more careful about what I wish for. This time my wish will be simpler—just a little peace and quiet.

The End

The Foolish Merchant and the Greedy Camel

(a retelling of an Arabic tale)

Puppets needed:

Man

Camel

Prop:

tent (optional)

NARRATOR: Once upon a time in the desert in the Middle East, a merchant set up his tent for the night. As he was arranging his pillows to sleep on, he saw the flap of his tent open slightly.

(*Camel and man enter*)

CAMEL: Oh, Master, Master!

MERCHANT: Yes, what do you want, Camel?

CAMEL: Nothing important, Master. It is just that I, your faithful camel, am getting rather chilly out here in the desert.

MERCHANT: Well, what is that to me? You are a beast of burden. You should be used to the nightly cold.

CAMEL: Oh, I am, Master, but I was wondering if I could ask a slight favor of you.

MERCHANT: Go ahead and ask; I am awake now. What is it?

CAMEL: Well, I wondered if I could just put my nose inside the tent to warm up a bit.

MERCHANT: I suppose that wouldn't hurt anything. Sure, but just your nose. It is a small tent, after all. Good night now.

NARRATOR: So the camel put his nose in the merchant's tent. A little later in the evening, the camel made a noise to get the merchant's attention.

CAMEL: Humpf. Humpf.

MERCHANT: What is it now, Camel?

CAMEL: Oh, nothing much, Master. I just wondered if I could put my whole head in the tent. It would be a lot warmer for me.

MERCHANT: Oh, I guess so. It's all right for you to put your whole head in the tent. Just let me sleep.

NARRATOR: So the camel put his whole head in the tent and was warmer that night. Then the next night, the camel made that noise again to get the attention of the merchant.

CAMEL:	Humpf. Humpf.
MERCHANT:	Yes, Camel, what is it now? Your head is now in the tent. What more do you want?
CAMEL:	I was happy with my head in the tent, but I was just wondering if you would object to my putting my front legs in the tent. I think that would make me more comfortable.
MERCHANT:	Well, I guess so. Your legs and your head, huh?
CAMEL:	Yes, Master. I'm sure I would be much more comfortable.
MERCHANT:	All right, now leave me alone.
NARRATOR:	So the camel put his front legs and his whole head in the tent. Later that night, the merchant heard the camel once again.
CAMEL:	Humpf. Humpf. Master, please wake up.
MERCHANT:	Huh? What is it now, Camel?
CAMEL:	Well, it's just that I am not very comfortable yet with just my head and front legs in the tent. I need to be completely inside the tent in order to lie down comfortably.
MERCHANT:	Well, I'm sorry, Camel, but there is no room in here for the both of us. The tent is just not big enough for us both to lie down.
CAMEL:	Yes, I realize that, Master, but . . . I have been thinking about that, and there is only one thing I can think of to do.
MERCHANT:	Yes?
CAMEL:	You will just have to leave the tent and let me have the whole tent to myself. I am after all the one doing all the hard work. I am the stronger one here, and I need my night's sleep.
NARRATOR:	And so the camel kicked the foolish merchant out into the cold night, while he, the camel, slept in the nice warm tent. (*Camel kicks the man out of the tent*) What is the moral of this story? Perhaps it is that there is proper behavior for everyone and everything. What may start out as an innocent enough exception may prove to be just the beginning of a major problem. You see, sometimes when you give some people an inch, they may try to take a mile. So, it is best sometimes to keep other people's noses out of your business.

The End

Fox's Sticky Santa Cake

(a retelling of "Brer Rabbit and the Tar Baby")

Puppets needed:

Fox

Rabbit

Prop:

Santa figure—stuffed Santa

NARRATOR: Old Brer Fox had had it! He was sick and tired of being tricked by Brer Rabbit. This time was going to be different. He had a plan—a foolproof plan to catch that rabbit once and for all.

FOX: *(Enters)* There's only one thing that I'm waiting to eat for my holiday dinner. Nothing compares with a tasty rabbit. I like mine with just a smidge of garlic and a lemon sauce, roasted over a real slow flame. Yum, yum. Well, it's time to try my scheme to snare that little pest of a rabbit so that I can cook him for my dinner. Here's my plan: I have baked up a very ooey, gooey cake smeared in thick honey in the shape of Santa Claus. I'm going to place Santa in the path of that Brer Rabbit. I know that old rabbit and how he likes nothing better than gabbing all the time. When he tries to have a conversation with Santa, that rabbit is going to be in for a big surprise. For once, he will be all stuck up. We'll see who gets caught now.

NARRATOR: So, as part of Fox's plan, Fox had put Santa smack-dab in the middle of the road. Rabbit wouldn't be able to miss him, and he wouldn't be able to resist talking to him either. *(Fox puts out Santa cake onstage)* Fox waited and waited for Rabbit to come walking down the road. Finally he spotted Brer Rabbit coming, and Fox hid in the bushes.
(Fox hides on other side of stage)

RABBIT: *(Enters)* Well, would you look at that! Santa as big as life right here in the middle of the road. Must have caught you getting ready to deliver gifts. I am plumb tickled to see you, Santa, seeing as how close this is to Christmas. I've been wanting to talk to you to tell you what I'd like for Christmas.

NARRATOR: Santa says nothing.

RABBIT: How's it goin', Santa? How are you feeling? Elves keeping you pretty busy? Care to shake my hand?

NARRATOR: Santa still says nothing.

FOX:	*(Whispers from hiding place)* Going good. I'm sure fooling him with that Santa cake. Santa's saying nothing. Ha, ha.
RABBIT:	I said, "Hi, there, Santa." Not very friendly are you? Kind of stuck up, huh?
FOX:	*(Whispers)* Not as stuck up as you are going to be!
RABBIT:	Why don't you answer me? I've been nice and not naughty all year long waiting for you. I think that I need to teach you some good manners.
NARRATOR:	Rabbit decided to get Santa's attention by smacking him upside his head, so he reared his paw back and gave Santa a good punch.
RABBIT:	*(Punches Santa)* How do you like that, huh, Santa? Oh, no. My paw is stuck. You let me go, you big bully. Give me back my paw!
NARRATOR:	But Santa cake still said nothing, and Rabbit's paw was good and stuck. Fox just laughed to himself.
RABBIT:	I think I am going to have to get nasty now, Santa. Time for another big punch.
NARRATOR:	And Rabbit raised his other paw and let Santa have it one more time.
RABBIT:	*(Punches Santa)* You are just terrible mean, Santa, keeping that second paw stuck on you too. I just don't get it, Santa. You're supposed to be a good guy. Aren't you going to answer me or give me back my two paws?
NARRATOR:	Santa still said nothing.
RABBIT:	Well, I'm about to give you a real lesson in politeness. I'm going to kick you real hard. That should get your attention. Here's goes. Now this may hurt some. *(Kicks Santa)*
FOX:	*(Whispers)* Hurt *you,* you mean, not Santa.
NARRATOR:	And Rabbit got his foot stuck in Santa as well. Fox finally came out of hiding.
FOX:	Well, if it isn't Brer Rabbit. All nice and stuck up, I see. All this noise and complaining because you got yourself caught on poor old Santa. I finally outsmarted you good this time, Rabbit. You know, I think it is about time for dinner.
RABBIT:	Thanks, Fox, but I'm not hungry.
FOX:	You still don't get it. *You* are my dinner. Let's see—how will I cook you? Roasted, fried, or stewed? Course I have to kill you first. Maybe if I threw you into the well and drowned you that would kind of clean you up before I cooked you?
RABBIT:	Sure thing. Good idea. The well it is.
FOX:	What do you mean by that?

RABBIT: I sure wouldn't mind a good dunking. I'm sticky and I'm thirsty. In fact, you are welcome to do just about anything to me except . . . oh, I don't want to even think about that.

FOX: What do you mean anything except what?

RABBIT: No, no, don't make me say it. I don't even want to talk about it.

FOX: Go ahead, Rabbit. Tell me now.

RABBIT: Well, the worst thing I can think of you doing to me would be to throw me in those prickly brambles. Anything but that!

FOX: Hmm. How about if I boil you in a pot of water instead?

RABBIT: Sure, that's OK. It's getting cold out here, and the hot water might kind of warm me up a bit. Just don't throw me in those bramble bushes.

FOX: You know, you have given me an idea. I won't drown you in the well or boil you in my pot; I'm going to do what you hate most. I've waited a long time for you, and you have tricked me too many times. I'm going to throw you in those prickly bramble bushes. See if you can fool this old fox now. Here goes.

NARRATOR: And Fox threw Brer Rabbit as far as he could into the patch of briars and brambles. *(Throws Rabbit)*

FOX: That should do it, huh, Rabbit? Nice and tenderized now?

NARRATOR: But all of a sudden, Brer Rabbit started to chuckle and then started laughing out loud.

RABBIT: Fox, I outsmarted you one more time. You did me a big favor. I was born and raised in those bramble bushes. Thanks for sending me home. Ha, ha. Merry Christmas! *(Exits)*

FOX: Just you wait, Brer Rabbit. I'll get you yet, and it won't be pretty next time. Oh, well, it is Christmastime, and I have worked up quite an appetite. I'll think pleasant thoughts. That Santa honey cake sure looks good enough to eat. I think I will. I'll just save Brer Rabbit for next year's dinner. Merry Christmas, everyone.

The End

Fox's Sweet Tooth

(a retelling of "The Gingerbread Boy")

Puppets needed:

Fox

Gingerbread Boy

Props:

NARRATOR: Once upon a time an old woman made herself an especially fine batch of gingerbread. She decided to make one large gingerbread boy and decorate him with raisin eyes and nose, red sugar mouth, and three buttons made of dates. When she was finished baking him, she thought she would have a nice dessert prepared for her company, but almost as soon as the oven door opened, out popped a gingerbread boy yelling.

GINGERBREAD BOY: *(Enters)* Run, run; go ahead and try. You won't catch me; I'm the Gingerbread Boy!

NARRATOR: Now since the old woman couldn't run, she didn't even try to catch the boy. No, she just started baking another batch of gingerbread. You probably remember that the Gingerbread Boy ran into a cow, a horse, and some farmers. At each of them he yelled.

GINGERBREAD BOY: Run, run; go ahead and try. You won't catch me; I'm the Gingerbread Boy!

NARRATOR: After he had run away from the old woman, a cow, a horse, and the farmers, the Gingerbread Boy was pretty proud of himself. In fact, he started to get a swelled head.

GINGERBREAD BOY: I can outrun anything and anybody. I'm the tasty, fast Gingerbread Boy! No one can catch me!

NARRATOR: Gingerbread Boy suddenly noticed a fox walking across a field. *(Fox puppet enters)*
When the fox started to approach the boy, Gingerbread Boy yelled tauntingly to him.

GINGERBREAD BOY: Run, run; go ahead and try. You won't catch me; I'm the Gingerbread Boy!

FOX: Silly Boy, why would I want to catch you?

GINGERBREAD BOY:

> Never had gingerbread before, huh? Well, I am mighty tasty for one thing. Of course I am a good runner as well. I outran the old woman, a cow, a horse, and some farmers, and I could outrun you too.

FOX: I suppose you could. I'm not the running type.

GINGERBREAD BOY:

> You mean that you don't want to chase me?

FOX: No. I'm just minding my own business walking along. See you, Boy.

GINGERBREAD BOY:

> Wait! I bet you'd like gingerbread. I'm sure that I am very tasty.

FOX: That may be, but I'm a fox, and I'm not really interested in desserts. Now, if you were a fried-chicken-nugget boy, a pork-chop boy, or a steak man, I might be interested.

GINGERBREAD BOY:

> All I can say is that you don't know what you are missing.

FOX: Maybe so. Well, off I go across the lake. By the way, how are you going to run across the lake? Can you swim?

GINGERBREAD BOY:

> No. I hadn't thought of that. I guess I might have some trouble getting across by myself.

FOX: Yeah. You could get a bit soggy, couldn't you? (Chuckles) Course I suppose I could help you out with that.

GINGERBREAD BOY:

> Could you? How?

FOX: Well, seeing as how I have to go across anyway, how about if you jump up on my tail and I'll wade across with you?

GINGERBREAD BOY:

> Thanks, I will. (Jumps)

NARRATOR: And the Gingerbread Boy jumped onto Fox's tail.

FOX: Gee, the lake is getting a bit deeper. Maybe you should jump on my back so you won't get wet.

GINGERBREAD BOY:

> OK. Here goes. (Jumps)

FOX: That's much better for now. Course if you were to jump up on my shoulders, you'd probably stay drier.

GINGERBREAD BOY:

If you think so. Here goes. (*Jumps*) It's a good thing I'm such a good jumper. Boy, I can run fast and jump too!

FOX: Isn't that something? Gingerbread Boy, my shoulders are getting a little achy. Do you suppose you could jump on my nose to give my shoulders a rest? Maybe you can't jump that far, though.

GINGERBREAD BOY:

Sure I can. I'll do that. (*Jumps*)

NARRATOR: The Gingerbread Boy jumped right on Fox's nose. It didn't take the Fox more than a second to open his big mouth wide. Then he threw his head forward quickly and *snap*—the Gingerbread Boy was history.

FOX: You know, he's right. That Gingerbread Boy was very tasty. And I didn't even have to run after him. He just came to me. Goes to show that even though that proud Gingerbread Boy may have been the fastest runner and maybe the best jumper around, he wasn't the cleverest boy I ever ran into. You know, I may develop a taste for gingerbread, after all. Got to get that recipe from the little old woman. Happy holidays, everyone!

The End

The Gift of the Two Brothers

(a retelling of a Jewish tale)

Puppets needed:

Two brothers

Prop:

wheat sheaves

NARRATOR: Once upon a time in ancient Israel there lived two brothers who both worked hard planting and harvesting their fields of wheat.

ELDER BROTHER:

(*Enters*) As the elder brother, I will go to my younger brother's home and give him some of my sheaves of wheat. I do not need all of my harvest, and my brother's large family could probably use some more food. (*Exits*)

NARRATOR: And so the elder brother left several bundles of wheat in his brother's barn and quietly went home. In the meantime, the younger brother also had a kind idea.

YOUNGER BROTHER:

(*Enters*) My poor older brother has no wife or children to help him with his harvest. Perhaps he would appreciate some of my plentiful harvest. (*Exits*)

NARRATOR: And the younger boy left several sheaves of wheat in his brother's barn and went home without telling his elder brother. Now when each brother went to his own barn the next day, guess what they each found? Each had exactly the same amount of wheat as they had before they had given some away.

ELDER BROTHER:

(*Enters*) How can this be? I still have the same amount of wheat. I must leave my younger brother some of this wonderful wheat that multiplies in the barn by itself. (*Exits*)

NARRATOR: And the younger brother found the same thing. There was no wheat missing.

YOUNGER BROTHER:

(*Enters*) I must share with my elder brother this wonderful good fortune. (*Exits*)

NARRATOR: So each brother brought the other some more sheaves of wheat and left the wheat in the barn without telling the other brother. On the third evening, when the brothers were each bringing the other some more wheat, they met each other in the fields.

(Both brothers enter)

ELDER BROTHER:

Oh, Brother, thank you for giving me wheat from your store of wheat. I appreciate your kindness, but you have a family to feed.

YOUNGER BROTHER:

Oh, it is I who should give you thanks, Brother. You gave me from the wheat you harvested by yourself. You know, we are both blessed.

NARRATOR:
And when wise old King Solomon heard about this story of the two loving, generous brothers, he decided that there in the field between the brothers' fields, he would build the Temple of Israel—for this spot would become a symbol of brotherly love and selfless generosity for all of Israel.

(Brothers shake hands)

The End

Goldi Makes a Friend

(a retelling of "Goldilocks and The Three Bears")

This play can be adapted to any holiday (e.g., Valentine's Day, Easter, Christmas).

Puppets needed:

    Goldi

    Little Bear

Props:

    note

    honey pot

    glue pot

NARRATOR: Once upon a time, long, long ago, Goldi Locks was back at home sitting in her parlor, feeling sorry for herself.

GOLDI: *(Enters)* I'm bored and I'm lonely. I'll never have anyone to play with. Why did I run away from the Bears' house? They must be very mad at me for breaking the chair, sleeping in their beds, and eating the porridge. I wish I had Little Bear for a playmate and friend. I wonder what I can do to make the Bears forgive me. Oh, it's hopeless!

NARRATOR: Goldi's dad and mom, Rusty and Amber Locks, tried to cheer her up, but it didn't work. Finally Dad just left Goldi a note. It read: "Stop your moping. That won't help. To have a friend you must first be a friend."

GOLDI: I guess Dad is right. First I have to be friendly. Maybe I can start with a peace offering to the Bears. It is close to Valentine's Day. Maybe I should start with a surprise Valentine's card.

NARRATOR: So Goldi found her way back to the Bears' house and left a surprise Valentine's card she had made herself for Little Bear.

GOLDI: *(Enters with envelope)* I hope Little Bear will read this card and like it. *(Goldi exits)*

NARRATOR: Soon Little Bear checked the mail and discovered a card addressed to him.

LITTLE BEAR: *(Enters)* Oh, boy, mail for me. It's a Valentine's card. It says:

> "You are cute
> You are neat
> I wish I had some porridge to eat.
> Guess who?
> (Signed) a would-be friend."

There's a chocolate egg in the envelope too. Yummy. I wonder who this would-be friend could be? I'll have to examine the clues. Whoever it is likes porridge. I wonder if it could be . . . I'll have to think about this. *(Exits)*

NARRATOR: And at home, Goldi wondered too.

GOLDI: *(Enters)* I wonder if Little Bear can figure out my note. I think I will try a second card tomorrow.

NARRATOR: And so the next day Goldi went back to the Bears' house. This time she left a second note and another little present—a small bottle of honey.

GOLDI: I'll hide and see if Little Bear likes this card and gift. *(Hides)*

NARRATOR: Soon Little Bear went to check the mail to see if another card had come, and sure enough, there was a second card for Little Bear.

LITTLE BEAR: *(Enters)* What a nice card. This one says:

> "Honey's sweet.
> You are too.
> I wish I had a friend like you.
> Guess who?
> (Signed) a would-be friend."

Oh, here's another gift too—a nice bottle of honey. I love honey, especially on my morning porridge. Who wrote this note and gave me the honey? I have to know. How did my would-be friend know I put honey on my morning porridge? Hmmmm.

(Both exit)

NARRATOR: And while Little Bear thought and thought, Goldi decided on a third and last note and gift. She would leave a pot of glue to fix the chair she had broken.

GOLDI: *(Enters)* Now I'll know for sure if Little Bear will forgive me. *(Exits)*

NARRATOR: Little Bear went to get his mail the next day.

LITTLE BEAR: *(Enters)* Oh, goody. Another note. This time the note says,

> "Sorry that I broke your chair.
> Please forgive me, Little Bear.
> Now you know the one to blame.
> Goldi Locks is my full name."

So that's who it was who ate my porridge, smashed my chair, and slept in my bed—a girl named Goldi Locks. She does seem sorry, though. I think I'll look up the last name Locks in the phone book and see where she lives. Then I can leave a note for her in her mail.

NARRATOR: Little Bear left a note for Goldi in her mailbox. Goldi was in for a big surprise when she checked her mail.

GOLDI: *(Enters)* Great. An answer from Little Bear. A note addressed to me! It says:

> "Father Bear has fixed my chair.
> Sorry that you had a scare.
> I can come outside to play.
> Ask your Mom if it's OK.
> (Signed) Little Bear."

(Goldi exits)

NARRATOR: Goldi was so glad. She raced inside to tell her mom and dad. She decided to write Little Bear one more note. Instead of leaving it in the box, though, Goldi was going to deliver this one in person.

(Goldi and Little Bear enter)

LITTLE BEAR: *(Note in hand)* Hi, you must be Goldi. I loved your notes. Oh, thanks for another one. This note says:

> "Mama says that it's OK
> If I go with you to play.
> Now we don't need notes to say
> We'll be friends for real today."

NARRATOR: And so that's how Goldi Locks and Little Bear finally became good friends. And do you know something? Goldi was never lonely or bored again.

The End

The Guardian Stone Lion

(a retelling of a Tibetan tale)

Puppets needed:

Two brothers

Lion puppet (left onstage to be the stone lion)

Prop:

bucket

NARRATOR: Once upon a time in Tibet there lived two brothers who were farmers. They were very different from each other. The older brother was conniving and greedy, while the younger brother was kindhearted and generous. The older brother was always jealous of his younger brother's good nature, so one day he ordered him out of the house.

(Both brothers enter)

OLDER BROTHER:

You must go. I can't take care of you any longer. You are just bringing our family fortunes to ruin. You must go and make your fortune by yourself. I wash my hands of you.

YOUNGER BROTHER:

Oh, Brother, I will go at once. I will try to make good on my own from now on. I will take our mother with me.

(Both exit)

NARRATOR: And so the younger brother and his mother left their home and headed into the open country. Finally, the boy found a small abandoned hut to live in for a while. He cleaned up the hut, cut wood, and settled in. The next day he went out early to cut more wood and sell the wood at the market. For several days he cut wood and sold it. One day, as the boy went further and further up a hillside to find more wood, he came to a stone lion carved into the side of the hill.

(Lion puppet enters)

YOUNGER BROTHER:

(Enters) This must be a guardian lion of the hillside. I should like to offer him some tribute for allowing me to find wood to sell from his mountainside.

NARRATOR: And the next day the boy cleaned off the statue and put fresh flowers in front of the stone lion. Suddenly the lion began to speak.

LION: Who are you? Why do you put flowers in front of me? Why do you do me this honor?

YOUNGER BROTHER:

I am just thanking you for allowing me to cut wood on your hillside.

LION: It has been quite a long while since I have been so honored. I will do you one more favor if you will come here again tomorrow with more flowers. Bring me an empty bucket. I will fill the bucket with pieces of gold for you and your mother. I have one warning, though. If even one gold coin falls from the bucket, you will lose it all. So don't be greedy. Tell me to stop before the bucket is completely full.

YOUNGER BROTHER:

Thank you, Lion. I will be back. *(Both Lion and Younger Brother exit)*

NARRATOR: And the next day the boy brought a bucket and flowers to the lion. The lion started to fill the bucket with gold. When the bucket was about three-quarters full, the boy yelled for the lion to stop. Now, with all this gold, the boy and his mother could afford a fine home. They were able to live quite happily. After a while, the older brother heard of his younger brother's good fortune. When he heard that the stone lion on the hillside had given the boy a bucket full of gold pieces, the older brother made up his mind to find that same lion and demand money for himself.

(Lion enters)

OLDER BROTHER:

(Enters) Are you the stone lion who gave my brother all those gold pieces?

LION: Yes, I am.

OLDER BROTHER:

Well, please do the same for me. I too need money. In fact, I need it more than he does, and as the older brother I deserve the money more than he does.

LION: I will do you the same favor I did for your brother. Bring a bucket tomorrow and I will fill it with gold, but you must stop me before the bucket is completely full. If even one piece of gold drops to the ground, you will lose it all. You must not be greedy.

(Older Brother exits)

NARRATOR: The next day the brother brought the empty bucket.

OLDER BROTHER:

(Enters) Here, Lion, you can fill it now for me.

NARRATOR: And the lion started filling the bucket with gold pieces. The bucket was filling up to the top, but the brother refused to say stop. Finally one piece fell to the ground. When the older brother reached for the single gold piece, suddenly the lion grabbed hold of the brother's hand in his mouth.

OLDER BROTHER:
(His arm is in the mouth of the lion) Oh, please, Lion, let me go. You can't blame me for wanting the gold my brother has.

NARRATOR: When the lion started to answer back, he opened his mouth and the brother got his arm free. *(Older Brother exits)* The older brother ran away as fast as he could, taking the empty bucket with him. As for the younger brother, he continued to share his good fortune with his neighbors and even with his older brother. And that bucket of gold? For some reason, no matter how much the young boy spent or gave away, there was always more gold. The younger brother never needed to go to the lion again, but every week he placed flowers at the lion statue. After all, he owed the guardian lion many thanks.

(You can have the lion take a bow)

The End

Hansel and the Witch

(a retelling of "Hansel and Gretel")

Puppets needed:
Hansel
Witch

Prop:
gingerbread house (optional)

NARRATOR: Once upon a time there was a clever boy named Hansel who lived with his father, his sister Gretel, and his stepmother in a little cottage in the woods. Hansel's father had lost his job, and the family was very poor; in fact, they were so poor that his father worried that they would not have enough food for the next meal. One morning after Hansel heard his father and stepmother arguing about money, Hansel decided to do something himself about the family problems. He said good-bye to his sister and quietly sneaked out of the house to seek his fortune. Hansel wandered around for three days in the woods until he came to a small clearing in the trees. There he spotted a strange little cottage. It looked like a big gingerbread house.

HANSEL: *(Enters)* I wonder who lives in this house? My goodness, the sides of the house seems to be made of bread, and the roof looks like frosted cake. The windows appear to be made of sugar. I'm so hungry that I am going to taste a few bites of the windows.

NARRATOR: As Hansel took a bite of a window, he heard a voice call out.

WITCH: Gnaw, gnaw, nibble, nibble, sounds like a mouse. Who's that nibbling on my house?

HANSEL: I must be hearing things. Maybe it's the wind blowing. I'll try a bit of the roof now. I am so hungry, I'll eat anything.

NARRATOR: As Hansel ate, the door of the cottage opened and a witch came out.

WITCH: *(Enters)* Well, lookey here! A little boy. How lovely! Do come inside and have a meal with me. You are hungry enough to eat my house, huh? Heh, heh. *(Cackles)*

HANSEL: I'm sorry if I bothered you. Thank you for your offer of food. *(Hansel walks across stage to house prop)*

NARRATOR: And Hansel stepped inside the neat little cottage. The witch served Hansel a filling meal.

HANSEL:	That was delicious. How can I repay you for the fine meal? You see, I haven't eaten in days.
WITCH:	We'll soon change that. Got to get you fattened up. *(Cackles)* Well, you can sleep upstairs. There's a bed ready for you. See you in the morning. Off to bed with you now.
HANSEL:	Yes, thank you again. See you in the morning. *(Exits)*
NARRATOR:	Now, when Hansel fell asleep and started snoring, the witch began her meal planning. You see, Hansel was to be on the week's menu.
WITCH:	Oh, goody, fresh young boy! Nothing like that to eat. I haven't had a tender young child in, let's see, a week or two. *(Cackles loudly)* I just have to fatten him up a little and then roast him slowly for a few days. It gives the boy a better flavor, and I'll have a chance to get all my side dishes ready.
NARRATOR:	Now Hansel woke up when he heard the witch's cackle. He heard her plan to eat him. For a few days, he acted as if nothing was wrong. He ate the witch's meals and helped her with her cooking and other household chores.
HANSEL:	*(Enters)* May I help you with something else around the cottage?
WITCH:	Yes, my dear. I think it is time. I am just about ready to start a casserole. How about if you creep in the oven and check the temperature for me? It should feel hot to you but not hot enough to burn you. I believe in slow cooking for full flavor. *(Cackles)*
HANSEL:	I'm sorry, but I'm a little big to step in there by myself without help. Could you show me how you do it?
WITCH:	Silly boy. You just step on that stool like this and open the oven door so that you can put your head in the oven.
HANSEL:	How far do I have to go in the oven?
WITCH:	As far as you can. Here I'll step in further and show you. *(Goes offstage)*
NARRATOR:	And when the witch was in the oven as far as she could go, Hansel gave her a little push and closed the oven door tightly. The witch, not Hansel, was slow cooking.
HANSEL:	Thank goodness that takes care of the old witch. She won't need to fix any more casseroles. It's time for me to be on my way. *(Exits)*
NARRATOR:	As Hansel looked around the cottage to get his things, he found bags of jewels hidden in every cupboard. Hansel gathered as many as he could and headed home. When he reached his home, he gave his father the jewels. His stepmother had already left home. She didn't want to be poor and hungry anymore. Gretel and Hansel's father welcomed the boy

back. And all three of them lived happily together. They were never poor or hungry again. As for the witch? No one ever heard from her again. In fact, her whole gingerbread house went up in flames one day. They say the heat from the oven cracked the house into crumbs.

HANSEL: *(Enters)* Now the witch can no longer hurt anyone. I agree with one thing that she told me, however. Sometimes slow cooking does bring out the flavor. She surely was a good cook. I'm just glad I wasn't the main dish.

The End

How Rabbit Lost His Long Tail

(a porquoi tale)

Puppets needed:
Rabbit
Mother Rabbit

Prop:
Sun (optional)

NARRATOR: Once upon a time Rabbit lived in the woods with his mother. He was a hard worker, going out hunting every day early in the morning so that he could find enough carrots and lettuce for them to eat. He also brought home some skins for his mother to dry so that they would have some protection against the winter chill. Rabbit was vain about one thing—his lovely, fluffy, long tail. He always took care not to get that tail caught in the brambles when he went out to hunt. One day Rabbit brought a whole basket of carrots and lettuce for his mother. He even had a few skins for her to dry on top. *(Rabbit enters)*

MOTHER: *(Enters)* Hi, Son. What a nice large basket of carrots and lettuce you have for us to eat. You must have had a good day. What's wrong? You look like you are upset about something.

RABBIT: I am, Mother. Even though I am up early in the morning every day so that I can find the best vegetables for us to eat and so I can check my traps, someone always beats me to it.

MOTHER: What do you mean, dear? How do you know that someone is there before you in the woods?

RABBIT: I know because when I look between the trees I see his long tracks. They are like long black lines. Whoever makes those tracks has awfully long feet.

MOTHER: Long tracks, huh? There is only one thing you can do. You must get up and start hunting an hour earlier. Maybe then you can beat whoever it is.

RABBIT: I guess I can do that. I'll start tomorrow at about 5:00 a.m. instead of 6:00 a.m. I'm going to brush my tail out a bit and then get to bed early.

MOTHER: OK, dear.
(Mother Rabbit and Rabbit exit)

NARRATOR: Well, Rabbit got an earlier start the next day, but guess what? There were those long dark tracks in the path once again. When he got home, Rabbit was cross and tired. *(Enters)*

MOTHER: *(Enters)* How was your day today, dear? Get there before anyone else?

RABBIT: Not so good, Mother. Here I took your advice and left home a whole hour earlier than usual, and someone still beat me to it. I saw the dark tracks again. What can I do?

MOTHER: There's only one thing for you to do. You should probably leave home even earlier. I'll wake you up at 4:00 a.m. this time and have a good breakfast ready for you to eat before you go.

RABBIT: OK, I'll try it once again. *(Mother Rabbit and Rabbit exit)*

NARRATOR: So Rabbit got up even earlier and went into the woods to hunt. Then he noticed yet again that those black tracks were there before him. This time Rabbit was really mad.

(Mother Rabbit and Rabbit enter)

MOTHER: I can see by your expression that you didn't get into the woods first, huh, dear? Maybe you should try getting up earlier still.

RABBIT: I don't want to get up any earlier. I'm up so early now that I can barely keep my eyes open.

MOTHER: Then how will you ever find out who it is that is there before you making those long dark tracks in the path?

RABBIT: I think I have an idea, Mother. I am going to fashion a big trap to catch the creature. That should work.

MOTHER: I don't think you should do that, dear. What if what you trap is a huge animal? It could be dangerous for you.

RABBIT: I'll be careful, Mother. This is the only way I can think of to find out who is making those tracks. Don't worry; I'll fashion a good strong trap and set it today. *(Mother Rabbit and Rabbit exit)*

NARRATOR: And Rabbit made and set his strong trap in the woods. In the early morning, he hopped out to the woods to see if his trap had anything in it. When he got to the trap, he saw that the woods were very bright and hot. You see, he had trapped the Sun. Rabbit was scared and hopped home as quickly as he could.

(Mother Rabbit and Rabbit enter)

RABBIT: Oh, Mother, I should have taken your advice and not set the trap. You know who was making those tracks in the woods?

MOTHER: No, dear.

RABBIT: It was the Sun making shadows with the trees. Now the Sun is caught in my trap. What should I do? What do you think the Sun will do to us?

MOTHER: If you don't free the Sun right away, the Sun will get so mad that he will burn us all up with his heat. You've got to free him from the trap.

RABBIT:	But it's so hot, Mother. I don't know if I can get close enough to open my trap.
MOTHER:	You must try, Son. Good luck. *(Mother Rabbit and Rabbit exit)*
NARRATOR:	And so Rabbit hopped back to the woods. As he got closer to the trap, it got hotter and hotter and brighter and brighter. At last he was near enough to spring the trap. The Sun lifted itself into the sky, but as it arose, it brushed against Rabbit's long, beautiful tail, singeing it nearly off. All that was left was a little puff tail. Rabbit went home with a little burnt stub of a tail.

(Mother Rabbit and Rabbit enter)

RABBIT:	Ow! That really stings!!
MOTHER:	Son, what happened to your beautiful long tail?
RABBIT:	I guess the Sun caught me after all. Oh, well, Mother, at least I don't have to get up so early in the morning anymore.
MOTHER:	And your tail may not be long and furry anymore, but it is kind of cute. I think that that's what I'm going to call you from now on—Little Cottontail.
NARRATOR:	And do you know that's why to this day rabbits still have little puffy tails. That old Sun has a long memory.

The End

Jenny and the Beansprouts

(a retelling of "Jack and the Beanstalk")

Puppets needed:

    Jenny
    Giant

Props:

    piece of paper
    beanstalk (optional)

NARRATOR: Jenny and her mother lived in a small cottage near the edge of the woods. It was a modest cottage, and Jenny and her mother had to struggle to get by. Jenny was a great cook, even though she was still a young girl. She could make a good-tasting meal from whatever was available in the pantry. Their garden in the backyard was always filled with vegetables, particularly green beans. They almost seemed to be growing wild. She and her mother ate a lot of green beans—green bean casserole and green beans added to various stews. They also liked bean sprouts, especially as a topping for the salads Jenny whipped up from garden greens. One day Jenny was dusting an old small harp that had sat on the mantle for as long as she could remember. Mother wouldn't part with it even though all the strings had been broken for quite a while. As she put the harp back, a sheet of paper fell out. It had been taped to the bottom of the harp. Jenny read the sheet aloud.

JENNY: *(Enters with letter)* It says: *(She reads)*

If you have found this note then you are probably thinking of tossing away one of my stolen treasures. Let me start at the beginning. I am Jack, also called Jack and the Beanstalk because of my by-now-famous dealings with a former giant. It happened long ago in my youth when I foolishly traded our prize cow for a handful of seeds. Mother threw them out of the window when I got home from the market and gave me a good thrashing. The next day, though, the seeds had taken root, and a huge beanstalk had grown up to the sky. I climbed up the stalk and found a home where a giant lived who loved to eat boys. He had bags of gold, a magic hen that laid golden eggs for him, and a golden harp that played the most beautiful music. I stole one of his bags of gold, his magic hen, and that harp and climbed down the stalk. When he started to climb down after me, I cut down the stalk, and he fell into that huge crater that I'm sure is still there in the yard. It didn't take me long to spend all the gold, and the hen stopped laying after a while. The harp strings gradually broke, one by one, until it no longer played any music. Because I had stolen all that money in my youth, I never took time to learn an honest trade, and I'm afraid I had very little left to live on in my later years. I have very little to leave my children now. Please forgive my foolishness. I did manage to save one thing for my descendants: attached to this paper is a packet of three seeds. I saved these for you. Plant them and nourish them carefully. Even though they are old, these are not ordinary seeds; they are magic seeds and should grow with the proper care. Maybe you will have better luck than I did. Learn to use your gifts wisely. Don't throw away your treasures like I did. Work hard. If things come too easily, you won't appreciate them.

Your ancestor,

Jack

NARRATOR: Jenny read and reread the letter and looked at those magic seeds.

JENNY: There's only one thing to do. I must plant these seeds and see what grows. *(Digs holes and plants seeds)*

NARRATOR: And so Jenny made three little mounds of earth and carefully poked a seed into each mound. It didn't take long for the seeds to sprout, but nothing unusual happened for several days. Jenny was beginning to doubt that the seeds were magic, but she watered them anyway. Finally one plant started growing and growing. One morning she looked out the window to see the stalk reaching all the way to the sky.

JENNY: I will follow Jack's lead and climb the beanstalk. Before I go, though, I am going to take one of our best laying hens with me and the broken golden harp. After all, Jack did steal from that giant's home. I may as well take one of my special casseroles, some fresh bread, and maybe some beansprouts to use in a salad. That will be a peace offering to the giant's family. *(Jenny exits)*

NARRATOR: Up and up she climbed, and Jenny finally reached land. In the distance she spotted a castle.

JENNY: *(Enters)* That must be the giant's home.

NARRATOR: At the gate she was met by a young giant who greeted her gruffly.

GIANT:	*(Enters)*

GIANT: *(Enters)*
Fee fi fo fum.
I see a young woman.
Be ye alive or be ye dead,
I'll grind your bones to make my bread.

What do you want here, young lady? Why did you climb up to my castle? Trying to steal what's left of the family treasures after that horrid boy Jack stole our gold so many years ago?

JENNY: Please, sir, I didn't know about all that stuff until very recently, and I've come to give your family back the stolen treasures. Here's one of our best laying hens to replace the hen that was stolen, and here's the broken harp. Maybe the harp has some sentimental value for your family.

GIANT: Hmm. What kind of trick is this? Well, thanks for their return. I can easily fix the harp with some new magic strings, and that chicken just needs a little of my special seeds to start her laying golden eggs. But enough of this. I am hungry. *Very hungry!* You would taste mighty good for dinner. You don't weigh much, do you? Still you'd be nice and tender. Not very old, are you, my dear?

JENNY: No, I'm still a young girl, but I do know a thing or two about cooking. Care to taste some of the casserole, breads, and beansprout salads I've brought for you?

GIANT: Sure. I can save you for the main dish.

NARRATOR: And so, Jenny unpacked all her foods and served them to the hungry giant.

GIANT: Mighty tasty. Could you do that again?

JENNY: Sure. Just show me to the kitchen.

NARRATOR: Jenny whipped up another dish or two for the giant.

GIANT: You aren't as worthless as that lazy Jack who stole from my grandfather. Maybe I'll just let you live and keep you here as my cook. Sound good to you?

JENNY: I'm afraid not, Giant. You see, I have a mother waiting for me. But I tell you what. If you let me go back home, I'll bring you more food every day for three days. Is that a deal?

GIANT: I guess so, if you promise to keep the meals coming.

(Both exit)

NARRATOR: And every day for three days, Jenny prepared special meals and climbed up the beanstalk to deliver them.

(Both enter)

GIANT: You know I may have misjudged you and your family. You are really a great cook, and you have kept your word to me. For your reward, I am going to give you back the hen you brought me that first day. However, this time she will lay golden eggs and not just regular hen eggs. How about that?

JENNY: Thanks, Giant, but I'll take the hen as a gift just as she is. I'd rather she just laid regular eggs. You can't eat gold, you know.

NARRATOR: Jenny and the giant developed a real friendship. The giant never again ate another young boy or girl, and Jenny climbed up the beanstalk once a week and on holidays to cook for the giant. Both the giant and Jenny had a particular fondness for beans, since there was always a big supply ready for the picking on the beanstalk. And while Jenny and her mother never became rich, they decided they were both very happy just the way they were.

The End

King Birdsnest

(a retelling of "King Thrushbeard")

Puppets needed:

Princess
Young man (King)

Prop:

cloak for young man (King)

NARRATOR: Once upon a time there was a beautiful, proud princess who was very bad-tempered. She treated her servants badly and was scornful of everyone, especially the men who came to court to ask for her hand in marriage. No one was ever good enough for the princess. One day the king, her father, arranged a banquet to which he asked all the available single men in the area. As she was led into the hall with the men, the princess immediately began to criticize and make fun of each of them.

PRINCESS: *(Enters)* Oh, what am I to do? There is not a man among all of these who is acceptable. That one over there is much too pale—looks like he has the strength of a child; and that one has a neck the size of a tree; that one is so short that I would have a hard time finding him in a crowd; and that last one has the funniest-looking beard. Why it looks just like a bird's nest growing on his chin! I think I'll call him King Birdsnest. *(Exits)*

NARRATOR: Her father was so upset when he heard all the mean comments his daughter had made that he told her that he would award her hand in marriage to the first beggar who came to the castle. When a traveling fiddler came to the palace to entertain at court, the king told his daughter that she would have to marry that poor fellow.

(Enter Princess and young man)

PRINCESS: Well, I guess I have no choice. My father has spoken.

MAN: I will accept you as my bride, though it is certain that you have much to learn before you become my wife.

PRINCESS: *You* will accept me? I am a princess who has been well educated in court, and you are but a beggar.

MAN: Yes, and you must come with me now. We will go to my poor cottage to live. A palace is no place for the wife of a traveling musician.

PRINCESS: But I must pack all my things. I am not ready to go.

MAN:	You will need just the clothes on your back to live in our little cottage. Come.
NARRATOR:	While the girl cried out to her father for mercy, the king turned a deaf ear to the girl and watched both of them leave the palace. The man led the princess to the edge of the kingdom and through a large forest. After they had walked for several days, they finally came to a beautiful meadow.
PRINCESS:	Who owns these pretty lands?
MAN:	They all belong to the man you mockingly called King Birdsnest. Now please follow me to our small hut.
PRINCESS:	You mean these lands could have been mine if I had chosen that suitor?
MAN:	Yes, but instead you mocked him. Come, it is not far to the hut.
NARRATOR:	They came to a very small hut where the musician lived.
PRINCESS:	This is totally unacceptable. Where's the cook and the servant? I am used to being waited upon. I am hungry and tired after that great journey on foot. I'll have my meal and then go to bed.
MAN:	You must get used to the idea that your life has changed. I'm afraid there are no servants here. If you wish to eat, you must prepare the meal yourself.
PRINCESS:	But I don't know how. I've never had to do it before.
MAN:	I will help you at first. I have a good cookbook that you can use when I am not here to help. (*Man and Princess exit*)
NARRATOR:	For a few days the princess and the musician got along fairly well. He helped her learn all sorts of things around the house. At night they would sit by the fire, and he would play the fiddle to entertain her. Although the princess seemed to be adjusting to her new life, at the end of the day, she was extremely tired. She wondered how she could have stayed up all night at the palace with one party after another. One day the man talked to his wife at the kitchen table.

(*Man and Princess enter*)

MAN:	Although it has been fun for me to teach you some of your duties in the house, you have mastered them well by now and I need to get back to my own traveling work. It is time now, my wife, for you to contribute more to our household income. While I am on the road earning money, I suggest that you can spend your days at the marketplace selling the goods you have been baking. You will not want for company or conversation while I am gone, since you can stay there each day until all the goods are sold. (*Man and Princess exit*)

NARRATOR: The princess started to complain, but she was too tired. She just shook her head and started baking. The next several days she spent selling the baked goods that she had baked during the evening hours. Everything went well for her, and she made quite a bit of money for the baked goods, until one day she decided to leave her stall unattended for a moment while she looked at some things to buy in another booth. It was just for a brief time, but in that time, a thief came through the market and stole all her goods and her money. She went home very disappointed and ashamed of what her husband would say to her when he returned.

(Man and Princess enter)

MAN: I see that you had trouble today. You cannot even do a simple thing like selling bakery goods in the marketplace. What am I to do with you? Everyone knows that you cannot run off and leave your goods and your money at the marketplace. I guess we will have to find some other way for you to earn money for us. I have thought of a job that is perhaps more suited to you. I heard that there is an opening at the palace for a kitchen helper and cook. What do you think of that?

PRINCESS: To think that if I had not had so much pride I might have been living in that palace, not working in the kitchen as a maid.

MAN: Yes, that is true, but so much for idle wishes. Go to the palace and see if you can do that job. *(Man and Princess exit)*

NARRATOR: And for the next several weeks, the princess acted as a maid in the palace kitchen—cleaning, cooking, and waiting on the table at court. One day she was told that she would be helping to serve the wedding banquet of King Birdsnest and his new bride. She tried to hide in the corner so that the king and his bride would not see her. All at once King Birdsnest entered the banquet and walked over to her, reaching out his hand to take hers. She was scared and tried to run away from him.

(King, with a king's robe, and Princess enter)

KING: And who are you, my dear? You seem too lovely a woman to be working as a kitchen maid.

PRINCESS: I am only a scullery maid in your kitchen, Your Highness.

KING: And are you married?

PRINCESS: Yes, Highness, to a poor musician. He is on the road now trying to earn some money with his fiddling.

KING: Is he a good man? Do you love him?

PRINCESS: Yes, Highness, but we are very poor. I'm afraid that I am not worthy to be his wife, because I am ill prepared to help much with the expenses we have. I am not trained in any useful skill.

KING: My dear, I have a confession to make to you. I am King Birdsnest and also your musician husband and also the thief who stole your baked goods at the market. For love of you I disguised myself as your poor husband and the thief so that you could see for yourself your terrible pride. A good queen has to be loving and gentle as well as practical. I see that now you are a changed woman. Would you do me the honor of sharing the duties of my kingdom?

PRINCESS: You are right, Your Highness, I am a changed woman, and I will love you whether your title be husband or king. But what do I call you?

KING: First, my name is Edward. You can call me that or "husband." I don't even mind if you call me King Birdsnest. I have gotten fairly used to that title.

NARRATOR: And King Birdsnest and the princess lived very happily as king and queen of the kingdom. Never again was the new queen filled with pride—that is, about anything but her baking and her beautiful growing family. King Birdsnest and his beautiful sweet-tempered queen made sure that all of their children were trained by their mother in the art of baking and by their father in fiddling. Everyone who came to the palace was always treated to the smells of fresh baking and the happy sounds of a lively violin.

The End

King Midaswell and His Gold

(a retelling of the King Midas legend)

Puppets needed:

King

Daughter

Props:

NARRATOR: Once upon a time in a kingdom across the sea lived a king called Midaswell and his lovely daughter, Princess Justine. King Midaswell was once a happy and generous man who ruled his kingdom with justice and charity, but since his wife's death, he had become embittered and preoccupied with money. His only reason for living seemed to be to amass as much gold as possible. His chief of state was also his financial advisor. Everything the king touched seemed to turn to gold, and so King Midaswell was a very, very rich man. His only saving grace was his love for his daughter, Justine, who was as sensible and kind as she was beautiful.

(Both enter)

KING: Daughter, it is time for you to marry. I am going to send around a questionnaire for every young, eligible nobleman in the kingdom to fill out before he is considered as a possible suitor for you, Justine. I want to be sure that any potential suitor is rich enough to be worthy of you.

NARRATOR: Now Justine had her own ideas about the type of man she wished to marry. For her, being rich didn't matter. She had seen how unhappy riches had made her father. After her mother's death, she had often retreated to the palace kitchens to help the chefs and cooks and to observe all the preparations. She had developed a particular fondness for one of the cooks, the baker. He was a handsome, cheerful young man with a wonderful sense of humor. The only laughter she ever heard was in the kitchen.

JUSTINE: You needn't bother with a questionnaire, Father. I know the kind of person I would like to marry.

KING: You may think you know, Justine, but you are ignorant in the ways of the world. We must find someone worthy of the great wealth you will inherit one day—someone who will be wise in the ways of investment so your fortunes will grow—someone whose wealth can match yours. A merger—that's how I like to think of it—a merger of fortunes. With my questionnaire I can truly see if a man is worth our spending time considering him as a possible partner for you.

JUSTINE: But, Father, I would like the man I marry to be good and kind and have a sense of humor. I don't care that much about the money.

KING: You are such an innocent child, my dear. Father knows what's best for you. Just leave everything to me.

JUSTINE: May I see the list of questions you are asking on that sheet, Father?

KING: Of course, my dear. I certainly value your input on this matter. Now I have to go and check my stock market reports. There's always more money to be made by a clever man. See you at dinner. (Exits)

NARRATOR: Princess Justine was almost ready to cry. As much as she loved her father, she did not want to wind up being married to a man just like him—a man preoccupied with his money. Princess Justine started to read the king's questionnaire.

JUSTINE: (Reads questions)

1. Have you ever been under a magic spell and been turned into a toad?
2. Where are you living now?
3. Where do you see yourself living in the next five years?
4. Where were you educated?
5. What is your idea of a good time?
6. Have you ever had the opportunity of meeting Princess Justine?
7. Do you understand the workings of the market?
8. Do you diversify your stock holdings?
9. What is your best quality?

Perhaps I can help my friend, the baker, by filling out the questions for him. I will be truthful, but I just won't be completely exact in my responses.

NARRATOR: So Justine set to work answering the king's questions.

JUSTINE: For the first question of whether or not he was ever under a magic spell and turned into a toad, I can answer "definitely not," because the baker is just an ordinary man and not a prince. Lucky for him! Next is where he is living now. I can truthfully say, "in a palace." As for where he sees himself in the next five years, I can say again, "still in a palace." The next question asks where he was educated. That's easy, because my baker was sent to France by the king himself to learn to prepare all that fancy cooking. I'll write, "Educated in a fine school in France." How about the question of what's your idea of a good time? I'll write, "Making lots of dough. I like to watch my dough rising—doubling in size." Now for the question of whether or not I have met the princess. I will honestly write, "We have shared some great meals together." For the question about my understanding of the market, I'll put, "I check it every day." I don't have to say that he visits it to buy fresh eggs and butter every day. As for the question of whether he diversifies his holdings, I will write simply that "I never put all my eggs in one basket." Now, finally, I have to answer what my best quality is. I will say, "I am a hard and careful worker. I do nothing in a half-baked manner." There now, all done. I'll just leave this here for the king to read. *(Exits)*

NARRATOR: Sure enough, after reading carefully all the questionnaires that were returned, the king was most pleased with one of the questionnaires— the one Justine filled out for her baker.

(Both enter)

KING: By royal decree I order the noble suitor who filled out this questionnaire to be my choice as the marriage partner for my beloved daughter, Princess Justine. He sounds ideal. He's got to be very rich if he lives in a palace, and he is interested in what's really important in life—money— or "dough" as he quaintly puts it. I order you to marry this man, Justine.

NARRATOR: And surprisingly enough to the king, Princess Justine agreed to the marriage immediately.

JUSTINE: If that's your will, Father, I will happily consent.

(Both exit)

NARRATOR: It wasn't until after the wedding that King Midaswell realized that the dough the young man was interested in was the eating kind and that the market he visited was not the stock market. After the princess and her husband had their first child, the king's interests shifted over completely from money to his golden-haired grandchild, called Dora. The king nicknamed her " little nugget." The king also developed an interest in writing his memoirs for his little Dora to read later.

(Both enter)

KING: My new book is now ready to be published, Justine.

JUSTINE: Oh, Father, that is wonderful! What are you calling the book?

KING: It's called *The King and His Dough.*

JUSTINE: No, Father, not money again!

NARRATOR: But the king just laughed. He laughed a lot these days.

KING: Not that kind of dough, dear. This book has recipes in it.

NARRATOR: And King Midaswell; Princess Justine; her husband, the baker; and their little child, Dora, lived happily ever after. And they all had as much dough as they ever wanted or needed.

The End

The Magic Glass

(a retelling of a Japanese tale)

Puppets needed:

Man

Woman

Prop:

mirror

NARRATOR: Once upon a time in a remote village in old Japan lived a young tailor with his wife and small daughter. Since the young man was a tailor, every few months he had to go far away to the big city to buy more materials and supplies for his work. One day he bid his wife and little daughter good-bye and set off for the city. While he was getting his materials, he decided to buy his wife a surprise—a wonderful piece of crystal on one side and frosted silver on the other, set in a lovely carved wooden frame. It was a mirror, and his wife had never even seen one before. When he gave it to his wife, she looked into the glass.

(Both enter)

HUSBAND: What do you see when you look into the crystal, my dear?

WIFE: Why, it is marvelous! I see a lovely young woman who changes expression and moves as I do. How can this be? Is it a magic glass?

HUSBAND: Not magic, my love, but a treasure nonetheless. It is called a mirror, and the lovely woman you see is you yourself. When you look into the glass, your own beauty is reflected back to you.

WIFE: Thank you, Husband. It is a treasure indeed, and I will pack it away with our finest things.

(Both exit)

NARRATOR: The family lived happily together for many years as their young child grew up. Her mother didn't bring the wonderful mirror out often so that the young girl would not grow vain and proud of her own good looks. One day, however, the mother felt ill and realized that she might not live too much longer. It was time to show her daughter the magic glass. Before she died, she left a note for the girl telling her daughter to look into the mirror twice every day, once in the morning and once in the evening. That way the girl would always know that her mother was looking after her, even in death. Every day the daughter looked into the mirror to see and to speak with her beloved mother.

(*Girl—can be the same puppet as for the mother—enters*)

GIRL: (*Looks into glass*) Mother, I have done all my duties today. Please give me the blessing of your smile and love for this evening.

NARRATOR: And so the girl grew up comforted by her mother's continuing love and smiles. One day her father saw his daughter speaking to the image in the mirror.

(*Man enters*)

HUSBAND: Why are you talking into the mirror, Daughter?

GIRL: Oh, Father, it was my mother's last wish for me to see her face every morning and every evening in this glass so that she can continue to watch over me, even in death.

HUSBAND: Oh, my dear daughter, then truly this is a magic piece of glass—a magic mirror that will always reflect the beauty of your mother's heart in you.

NARRATOR: And the father never did tell his daughter that day by day the face she saw in the mirror was her own lovely face—a mirror of her beautiful mother's undying love.

The End

Old Babouscka

(a retelling of the Russian legend)

Puppets needed:

Old woman

King

Props:

NARRATOR: Once upon a time, a long time ago in the cold of a Russian winter, there was a very old woman who lived alone in a little hut. *(Woman enters)* She worked all day long cleaning her hut and taking care of herself, for she lived far away from any neighbors in a very cold part of the country. She hardly had any visitors, especially in snowy weather when the roads were blocked with powdery snow. One day she opened the door of her hut to see in the distance a line of people coming toward the hut. As the people got closer, she could make out three men on camels leading the procession. They must be very wealthy kings to be clothed in such fine robes, she thought.

WOMAN: I see a whole line of men on camels coming this way. Whatever could they be doing in our remote little section of Russia? These men seem important. What shall I do? I have so little to offer a traveler in my poor hut.

NARRATOR: Before long, the woman heard a knock on her door. *(King enters)*

WOMAN: Oh, sir, what may I, a poor woman, do for you?

KING: Madam, do not be afraid. We saw the light from your hut and decided to stop for a while on our long journey. As you know, the weather is very cold, and there are not many places we can stop in this country.

WOMAN: What type of journey are you on? What are you seeking?

KING: There are three of us. We are kings from far-off countries. We have seen a star in the East and are following it to find a little town called Bethlehem where a wonderful child has just been born.

WOMAN: All of this for finding a newborn child? What makes this child so special?

KING: We travel so far because we have heard that although he is a tiny baby, he is also a great king. We have come to offer him our gifts of gold, frankincense, and myrrh. Will you come with us on our pilgrimage to find this young king?

WOMAN: I would like to, but I am old. I never leave my house, because I have so much to do. Maybe I could see the baby later. In the meantime, you are welcome to stay in my humble hut as long as you wish. I will start right away to make some food for our dinner. It will not be fancy food, but I hope you will join me for dinner. I can also offer you a warm place to sleep for the night.

KING: Thank you for your kind offer. We would be happy to eat with you and stay for the night, but we must be off early in the morning to continue on our journey. We have so far to go. *(King and woman exit)*

NARRATOR: And the three kings ate with the old woman and spent the night in her hut. When the old woman woke up the next morning to make breakfast for the men, she discovered that the kings were already on their journey. They had left her a note and some money for her hospitality.

WOMAN: *(Enters)* Oh, they are all gone as they said and have even left me a gift for their visit. How kind they were, and how lonely it is without my company. Have I made a terrible mistake in not going with them to find the child? I am so sorry that I did not go with them. What have I done?

NARRATOR: The old woman could think of nothing else for days. One day she decided to leave her hut in order to follow the kings. Unfortunately, the kings had left days before, and no one could tell the woman which direction they were headed.

WOMAN: But I must find this child! How am I going to find him by myself? *(Exits)*

NARRATOR: The poor woman never did find the child king that the three kings were seeking. And so, for years, she wandered around visiting all the young children and bringing gifts to them, to see if she could find the right child. Even today, she brings little presents and candy that she makes to all the little children she visits during the holidays. So today in Russia, little children wait for a visit from this old woman, whom they call Babouscka. She continues to bring surprises to children wherever she goes, and to this day she is still looking for that one special child, that infant king.

The End

The Princess and Her Golden Ball

(a retelling of "The Princess and the Frog")

Puppets needed:

Princess
Frog
Prince

Prop:

golden ball

NARRATOR:	Once upon a time the youngest daughter of the king was playing outside in the palace gardens with a golden ball her father had given her for her birthday.
PRINCESS:	*(Enters)* This is a favorite piece of gold, because it was given to me by my father. I wonder if a ball of gold can bounce. I think I'll try it.
NARRATOR:	And the princess started to bounce the ball. On the third attempt, the ball fell into the garden well.
PRINCESS:	Oh, no, my golden ball has fallen into that old well. What can I do? Father will be furious with me for trying to bounce it. I know I can't get into the well by myself. *(Cries)* Oh, there is nothing for me to do. *(Cries)*
NARRATOR:	Well, the princess cried so hard that she couldn't stop. Suddenly she heard a strange voice calling to her.
FROG:	*(Enters)* Princess, Princess, why are you crying so? Perhaps I can help you. Is there anything I can do for you?
PRINCESS:	It's my golden ball. *(Sniffs)* I have lost it down a well. It was a special birthday gift from my father. It's a beautiful piece of gold, and I foolishly tried to bounce it. Oh, I am so miserable.
FROG:	You needn't be so sad. I think I can help.
PRINCESS:	You? You're just a frog. Whatever could you do?
FROG:	Well, I can probably fetch your ball for you out of the well. What would you do for me if I helped you out?
PRINCESS:	I would do whatever you'd like. I want that ball back. What could a frog like you want, anyway?
FROG:	Just one thing. I want to be your companion—I want to sit with you at the dinner table and eat from your dish. I want to rest with you in your bed.

PRINCESS:	But you are a frog. You can't be my companion.
FROG:	I've made up my mind. That's what I want from you. If you promise me that I can be your companion, I'll go into the well and get your ball.
PRINCESS:	Oh, all right. Whatever you say—just be quick about it. *(Frog exits)*
NARRATOR:	So the frog jumped into the well and brought up the princess's golden ball and gave it to her.

(Frog returns with ball)

PRINCESS:	My ball! My golden ball! Thank you, Frog. Got to run back to the palace for dinner now or I'll be late. Bye. *(Exits)*
FROG:	But Princess. . . . Wait! Remember your promise to me. *(Exits)*
NARRATOR:	But the princess had already run inside, leaving the poor frog behind. That night there was a terrible knocking at the palace gates. The princess guessed that it must be the frog she had left in the garden. When she explained to the king what she had promised to the frog, the king ordered her to let the frog in and keep her promise to him.

(Princess and Frog enter)

PRINCESS:	Oh, this is so disgusting. You insist on sitting next to me at the table.
FROG:	I'm sorry, Princess. I won't take up much space. I would like to sit right next to you, if you don't mind.
PRINCESS:	Well, I do mind. I can't eat with you sitting so near me at the table. Oh, all right. Come on, sit here.
FROG:	Thank you, Princess. Now would you please move your plate over a bit so that I can eat from your plate?
PRINCESS:	Oh, that's too much. I'm not going to eat anything with you touching the food on my plate.
NARRATOR:	But the king insisted that his daughter do as she had promised. When the meal was over, the frog spoke again to the princess.
FROG:	That was an excellent meal. Now you must be tired, Princess.
PRINCESS:	As a matter of fact, I am. It will be very good to get away by myself in my own bedroom.
FROG:	I'm afraid you won't be alone.
PRINCESS:	Why not? What do you mean, Frog?
FROG:	You must remember your promise to me. You promised me that you would let me sleep in your bed.
PRINCESS:	Now that's just going too far. You are a dirty frog. I don't want you messing up my nice clean satin sheets.

FROG:	But you promised. You must keep your word.
PRINCESS:	You are nothing but a horrible frog.
NARRATOR:	And the princess picked up the frog with two fingers and threw him hard on the floor. He slammed against the wall. (*Say "thump" loudly; both exit*) All of a sudden when the frog hit the wall, something strange happened. (*Poof!*) The frog seemed to burst open and a handsome young man appeared.

(Princess and man enter)

PRINCESS:	But who are you? Where is that awful frog?
PRINCE:	I am a prince from a nearby kingdom. I was under the spell of a witch until you broke the spell by throwing me on the floor.
PRINCESS:	I did? Did I hurt you?
PRINCE:	I think you helped me. You broke that wicked spell, after all.
NARRATOR:	And the prince stayed with the princess and her family in the palace for a month or so before he decided to ask the king for the hand of the princess in marriage. The king readily consented.
PRINCE:	And will you be my wife, dear Princess?
PRINCESS:	Yes, I will, Prince.
PRINCE:	Please accept then this engagement ring with all of my love.
PRINCESS:	My dear, it is a lovely ring in the shape of a little frog. I have no ring to give you in return, but I do have something precious to me that I will give you. Here, please accept my golden ball. I would not have it to give to you if you had not helped me.
PRINCE:	Thank you, my dear. Our bargain is almost complete now. Just one more thing. What would you have me promise you for this beautiful ball?
PRINCESS:	Only that you will love me forever.
PRINCE:	That is a promise that I can surely keep.
NARRATOR:	And the princess and the prince lived together happily for many years. The golden ball was placed in a special case in their bedroom as a symbol of their love. As a matter of fact, the princess wound up keeping her first promise to the frog after all, for she never ever took her frog engagement ring off her finger. It was her constant companion.

The End

The Princess and the Pea Test

(a retelling of "The Princess and the Pea")

Puppets needed:
   Prince
   Princess

Props:
   none

NARRATOR: Once upon a time in a far-off kingdom lived a prince whose old father was going to step down as king so that his son could become king. But there was one condition: the prince had to find a suitable princess to marry. It had to be a princess, and princesses were getting harder and harder to find. If one came to the castle to meet the prince, she still had to go through the old princess-and-the-pea test, and that meant at least one sleepless night. The problem was that two princesses had already visited the kingdom and had failed the pea test. Oh, they were really princesses, all right. They both were led to a bedroom with twenty mattresses piled on top of each other. On the top of the first mattress was a single pea. The first princess complained bitterly all night, and the next morning she just left the castle without even saying good-bye. The second princess stayed the night on the mattress too but the next morning rather rudely responded to the king and queen's question of how well she slept. Even if they were princesses, they were not the right kind of princesses to suit the king and queen for their son. Why, they were not even polite! One day a lovely young woman appeared at the castle. She was dressed very nicely, but she made no claims about being a princess. She didn't want to be welcomed just because she was a princess, so even though she was a real princess, she concealed that fact from the royal family.

(Both Princess and Prince enter)

PRINCESS: Good morning, Your Highness. My name is Iris, and I came to visit from a neighboring kingdom to tour your beautiful gardens. Would it be all right if I walked through your rose and iris gardens?

PRINCE: Certainly, Iris. I'll take you through them myself. My mother takes a great deal of pride in her flower gardens. Her roses and irises are special favorites of mine too.

NARRATOR: And the prince and Iris spent several hours walking and talking in the beautiful gardens.

PRINCE: Do you have to head back home today, or can you stay for a longer visit? We have plenty of rooms if you can stay with us for a while.

IRIS: I'd love to, Your Highness. It is a rather long ride back home. Thank you.

PRINCE: I'll ask someone to get your room ready then. Good night, Iris.

IRIS: Good night, Your Highness.

(Prince and Iris exit)

NARRATOR: And the prince quickly went upstairs with a freshly shelled pea and carefully placed it under twenty mattresses.

PRINCE: *(Enters)* Maybe she really is a princess and doesn't know it. You never know.

NARRATOR: In the morning, the prince was anxious to ask how Iris slept. Iris, however, knew about the pea test. All princesses do, after all. She decided to stall a little longer before she revealed her identity to see if she really liked the prince.

(Iris enters)

PRINCE: Iris, how lovely you look this morning. Did you sleep well?

IRIS: Oh, fine. As a matter of fact, I was sitting in that comfortable chair next to the bed reading, and before you know it, I was sound asleep.

PRINCE: The chair, huh? Didn't try the bed then?

IRIS: No, I'm afraid not.

PRINCE: Well, maybe tonight you can try the bed. It's one of the most comfortable beds in the whole castle.

(Prince and Iris exit)

NARRATOR: And the prince and Iris spent a second day together. This time they played tennis outside and then talked and talked. The prince found Iris very easy to talk to.

(Prince and Iris enter)

PRINCE: Tonight, Iris, remember to sleep in the bed. You'll get a better night's sleep on that.

IRIS: Good night, Your Highness.

PRINCE: Good night, Iris, and sleep well.

(Prince and Iris exit)

NARRATOR: The prince hurried upstairs to place several fresh, hard peas under all the mattresses, just in case Iris was a princess. The next morning he anxiously awaited Iris at the breakfast table.

(Prince and Iris enter)

PRINCE: So nice to see you, Iris. Did you sleep well last night? You're looking pretty today.

IRIS: Oh, yes, Your Highness. I slept very well. I started writing some letters on the couch and lost track of time. I guess I just fell asleep.

PRINCE: So you didn't try the bed yet, huh? Well, maybe you can try the bed tonight.

(Prince and Iris exit)

NARRATOR: The prince and Iris spent another day together, this time exploring the countryside, stopping at some little towns to look around. Mostly they just talked.

(Prince and Iris enter)

PRINCE: You know, it is funny how we have the same taste in reading and in music.

IRIS: Yes. I'm sorry if I have kept you from your palace duties these three days, but it has been so much fun being with you. I should leave tomorrow, though.

PRINCE: You have been a wonderful guest. It was a pleasure to have you to talk to. Please do try the bed tonight, Iris. Mother will be disappointed if you don't.

(Prince and Iris exit)

NARRATOR: So, the prince rushed upstairs to Iris's room. This time he had a whole handful of fresh, hard peas. He sprinkled them all on top of the lowest mattress.

PRINCE: *(Enters)* Oh, if only Iris were a real princess. She would make a wonderful wife and queen. *(Exits)*

NARRATOR: Next morning Iris came down for breakfast. She did sleep in the bed, but she got almost no rest, turning and tossing around on all those peas. She thought of telling the prince about her true identity, but she still wasn't sure he loved her for herself.

(Prince and Iris enter)

PRINCE: Good morning, Iris. You look a bit tired. Did you sleep well last night? Comfortable mattress?

IRIS: Thanks, Your Highness. It wasn't the fault of the mattress. I guess I had some things on my mind. I should be leaving soon.

PRINCE: Oh, must you go? We have such fun doing things together. It's just a shame that you are not . . .

IRIS: Not what, Your Highness?

PRINCE: Oh, nothing. It doesn't matter. How would you like to live here in the palace as my wife? Even if you're not a princess, you are still the most beautiful and interesting woman I have met. I love you. If I lose the throne, you will never get to be queen, though. Would that bother you very much?

IRIS: No, that wouldn't bother me at all. I would be happy to marry you, Your Highness, but I think you should ask my parents for permission.

PRINCE: Gladly. What are their names and address? I'll write immediately.

IRIS: They are King Frederick and Queen Isabelle.

PRINCE: But that makes you a princess then.

IRIS: I'm still the same person I was three days ago. Yes, I am a princess, but I wanted for you to love me, even though you thought I was just an ordinary girl. I wanted to see if you would love me enough to even give up the throne.

PRINCE: Sometimes things work out as well as they do in a fairy tale.

(They embrace)

IRIS: One thing, Prince, dear, would you mind taking the peas off my mattress? That's the worst sleep I have ever had.

PRINCE: Certainly, my love. From now on we'll keep the peas in the kitchen where they belong.

NARRATOR: Iris and the prince lived happily ever after. By the time their children were ready for marriage, the old pea test was a thing of the past. Whenever peas were served for dinner, however, Queen Iris and her husband the king just looked at each other and winked.

The End

A Promise to a Spider

(a retelling of "Rumpelstiltskin")

Puppets needed:

>Young woman
>Spider

Props:

>none

NARRATOR:	Once upon a time in a kingdom far away lived a queen who was very concerned that her son the prince find a good woman to marry. She was convinced that if her son were left to his own decision, he would make a poor choice. So, she proposed a trial for each of the young women that the prince showed interest in. The winner would get her son in marriage. Now the queen wanted a clever and hardworking wife for her son—someone who already knew a useful trade—not just an empty, pretty face. In that same kingdom lived a merchant who wanted his daughter to be the choice for the prince's wife. His daughter Sophia was already a friend of the prince, and the merchant thought of all the wealth he would have if his daughter became part of the royal family. The merchant brought the girl to the castle and ordered her to take the queen's trial. Sophia was ushered into a bare attic room and told that she must weave the most beautiful and finest silk thread into material that could be used for a wedding dress. All of this had to be done in one day's time. As Sophia sat in the room, she cried to herself. Looking around the bare room, she saw only a spider weaving a web in the corner of the room.
SOPHIA:	*(Enters)* I should clean that corner and get rid of that spider.
NARRATOR:	But before she could grab a cloth to dust away the spider, she heard the spider speak out to her.
SPIDER:	*(Enters)* If you spare my life and leave me in my little corner, I will reward you by helping you spin and weave the finest silk cloth you have ever seen or felt.
SOPHIA:	Thank you, Spider, for your offer. I will gladly spare your life.

(Both exit)

NARRATOR:	Together Spider and Sophia worked the whole day and into the night. By the next day the material was completed. Sophia took the cloth to the queen for her inspection. Although the queen was very pleased

with the lovely material, she was not through with her test of Sophia. This time she set Sophia to a second test. She was to make the material for the queen's dress for the wedding. It had to be of the finest silk, as fine as the wedding-dress material she had already woven. This too had to be completed in one day. So Sophia once again went back to the attic room and started to cry.

SOPHIA: *(Enters)* How will I ever weave more material for the queen's dress? *(Cries)*

SPIDER: *(Enters)* I can't help but hear your crying. Wasn't the queen pleased by the material we wove?

SOPHIA: Yes, she was so pleased with it that now I have to weave more material. It is for the queen's dress and must be of the finest silk—as fine as the material we have already woven. How am I going to do this all over again?

SPIDER: Well, if you make me a promise, I will help you once again. You must allow me and my descendants to live in peace in a corner of your home, wherever that home is. Do you promise?

SOPHIA: Yes, I will gladly promise you that if you will help me, I will always allow you to have your own corner to live in undisturbed.

SPIDER: Then let's get to work.

(Both exit)

NARRATOR: And the two set to weave the most beautiful silk fabric—even more soft and light than the material for the wedding dress. When the queen saw this material, she was surprised and pleased, but she had one final trial for the girl to pass. This time Sophia was to embroider with the most intricate stitches the material for the bodices of both dresses. The embroidery must be finished in one night. So Sophia went up to the attic once again.

SOPHIA: *(Enters)* Oh, what shall I do? First the material had to be woven and then it must be embroidered. I have never embroidered anything as delicate as that material. What if I ruin it?

SPIDER: *(Enters)* Perhaps you don't realize that I am an artist in embroidery. No one can match the fine, intricate stitches we spiders can make. This time, however, I have one more promise to extract from you. You must name your firstborn daughter after me, the lowly spider. I want my name known and honored in the kingdom. Will you promise me that?

SOPHIA: Yes, if I must. Please, let's get started on the embroidery.

SPIDER: One more thing. If you don't name the child after me, I will be forced to bite the baby and poison her. Just be sure that you keep your word to me.

(*Both exit*)

NARRATOR: And so Sophia and the spider embroidered both pieces of material with beautiful, intricate patterns and designs. When Sophia took the material with the lovely embroidery to the queen, the queen was amazed at its beauty. She finally gave Sophia her blessing to be married the next day to the prince. Sophia and her prince had a wonderful marriage, and for the first year they were very happy. Sophia learned in the next year, however, that she was expecting their first child. By now, Sophia had almost forgotten all about her promise to the spider, until the queen asked that the baby be named after her—Caroline—if the child was a girl.

SOPHIA: (*Enters*) Oh, what will I do now? How can I name my baby girl "Spider"? The queen would never permit that. No, that would never do.

NARRATOR: Now fortunately Sophia was a young lady who loved to read, particularly books on mythology. She remembered a myth about the most famous of Greek weavers by the name of Arachne, or *Spider* in Greek. In a few weeks, Sophia had a beautiful baby girl.

SPIDER: (*Enters*) Well, I have come to learn the name of your new baby. Will you call her "Spider" after me as you promised?

SOPHIA: I will keep my promise. Our baby girl's name will be "Caroline Arachne."

SPIDER: You know that is a lovely name—very classy in Greek. Thank you for keeping your word.

NARRATOR: From that point on, Sophia kept all her promises to the spider. She made sure that no one ever killed spiders in the kingdom. She also made sure that no one ever disturbed spiders in the corner of the palace dining room. The spiders in the kingdom made the child Caroline Arachne the most beautiful silk embroidered baby dresses. After a while, Sophia gave her baby girl a new nickname—after all Caroline Arachne was a mouthful to say. Her new nickname was—you guessed it— "Spider."

The End

Rooster Outfoxes Fox

(a retelling of a folktale)

Puppets needed:
Rooster
Fox

Props:
none

NARRATOR: One fine morning on MacDonald's farm, the rooster got up early. After all, he had to get everyone up with his cock-a-doodle-doo. He flew up to the top of the barn at his usual post and let out his loudest call.

ROOSTER: *(Enters on top of the stage)* Cock-a-doodle-doo! Wake up, everyone.

NARRATOR: Now, not only the farm animals heard the wake-up call. A fox that happened to be walking around the farm heard the rooster too. He wasn't interested in a wake-up call, though; he was thinking about his next meal, and that plump rooster surely seemed like a good possibility. Fox had to get that rooster off the barn and down on the ground so that he could catch him and eat him. He had a foolproof plan. A clever fox like him always had a plan. He walked over to the barn and called up to the rooster.

FOX: *(Enters)* Morning, Rooster. You are sure up early this fine day. Maybe it's because you've heard the good news.

ROOSTER: Good news? What good news?

FOX: Then you haven't heard, huh? It's really great news for all of us, not just good news.

ROOSTER: That's nice. What is this good, I mean great, news?

FOX: Well, beginning today, all the birds and the fish and other animals have promised to live together as friends. No more enemies, no more tricks, and no more arguments—just friends.

ROOSTER: Well, that does come as a surprise to me. Beginning today, huh?

FOX: Yes, no animal has to worry about being harmed by another one from now on. No more chasing or eating each other either.

ROOSTER: That sounds great, but I don't believe it.

FOX: Why don't you just come on down to the ground, and we can talk about it? It's too hard to explain it all to you when you are so far away.

NARRATOR:	Now, old Rooster was smart enough to know how sly and clever that fox was. Luckily Rooster had a plan of his own.
ROOSTER:	You know, Fox, I can see far and wide from my perch up here on the roof.
FOX:	That's great, Rooster. What do you see?
ROOSTER:	Well, for one thing, I can see some hound dogs off in the distance, running here as fast as they can. Must have picked up your trail, huh? Oh, I forgot, from now on all animals are going to live in peace.
FOX:	Really! Well, I must be off, Rooster.
ROOSTER:	So soon? Why? You still have to tell me more about the great news.
FOX:	Maybe some other time. I really have to run now. I don't know if the hounds have heard the message yet, you know. *(Exits)*
ROOSTER:	Sure, Fox.
NARRATOR:	And so the Rooster just crowed to himself one more time.
ROOSTER:	Cock-a-doodle-doo!
NARRATOR:	This time he knew that he had outfoxed old Fox, so he really had something to crow about.

The End

The Shoemaker and the Elf
(a retelling of "The Shoemaker and the Elves")

Puppets needed:

Shoemaker

Elf

Prop:

shoes (optional)

NARRATOR: Once upon a time in the Christmas season there was a poor shoemaker who had run out of money. Soon he would have to close down his small shop. He had only one piece of leather left to use to make a pair of shoes. Using this last piece of the leather, he cut out a pair of shoes so that he could sew them up the next morning. When he went to the workroom the next day to begin sewing the shoes, he found that a beautifully made pair of shoes was already completed on his worktable. They were sewn with perfect tiny stitches. A customer came in, saw the pair of shoes, and bought them on the spot. He paid a good price, since they fit him so well and were so beautifully made.

SHOEMAKER: *(Enters)* I am so happy. This sale means that I can afford to buy more pieces of leather. I think that I can get enough to make four new pairs of shoes. I bet I can sell the shoes too, since it is the Christmas season.

NARRATOR: And the shoemaker set to work cutting out four new pairs of shoes. By evening he had all of them cut out and ready to be sewn up. *(Shoemaker exits)* Next morning the shoemaker again had a surprise.

SHOEMAKER: *(Enters)* Why, I left the leather all cut out on my table, and now I have four beautifully sewn pairs of shoes to sell today. I've got to know whom to thank for this wonderful gift. How can I thank him enough? If I sell these beautiful shoes, I'll have plenty of money for Christmas presents for the children and enough money for a big feast for the holidays. I think I'll wait up all night to see if I can discover the kind person who helped me out. I'll just hide in the back of the room in a closet.

NARRATOR: As the shoemaker hid *(Hides)* and waited for the surprise person to come back and stitch up the new piece of leather, he saw an elf come in about midnight.

ELF: *(Enters)* Oh, good. A nice large piece of leather. I think I can stitch up another four or maybe five pairs of shoes for the good shoemaker to sell.

NARRATOR: And the elf set out to work.

ELF: Stitch them up as quick as can be. I'll sew them, oh, so carefully! And
no   one knows the maker's me! *(Exits)*

NARRATOR: Next morning, the shoemaker came to his table and found five pairs of
shoes completely sewn.

SHOEMAKER: *(Enters)* Now I know the person to thank. When I sell these shoes, we
will have lots of money. Since it's so close to Christmas, I know
something I can do for the elf. He must be cold without proper winter
clothing. I'll make a nice warm jacket for him, just his size.

NARRATOR: And the shoemaker sat down at his table and sewed up a heavy jacket
for the elf.

SHOEMAKER: Now that I am finished with the jacket, I am going to leave it out on the
table with a new piece of leather. I hope that the elf will see his present.
(Exits)

NARRATOR: When the elf came in later that night, he saw the wonderful warm little
jacket on the table. After he had sewn up the new piece of leather, he
looked at his new jacket.

ELF: *(Enters)* I guess the shoemaker must have liked the shoes I made for
him. What a nice gift he made for me in return. Now that the
shoemaker has seen me, though, I must leave, but my parting gift for
the kind shoemaker will be that every pair of shoes he makes will be
made well and will fit comfortably.

NARRATOR: And the elf went out singing.

ELF: My job sewing now is through. *(Singing)* Best of luck in all you do.
That's my Christmas wish for you! *(Exits)*

NARRATOR: And from then on the shoemaker worked hard and did very well.
Everyone knew of his fine workmanship. Each Christmas the
shoemaker left a Christmas present for the elf, and in the morning the
shoemaker always received a tiny, finely made ornament for his
Christmas tree. You see, elves never forget a kindness. Merry Christmas!

The End

Simplyella

Puppets needed:
  Simplyella
  Jerome

Props:
  none

NARRATOR: Once upon a time in a far-off land lived a young woman named Simplyella. Actually her real name was Ella, but Simplyella was what her two younger stepsisters tauntingly called her, making fun of her plain, short name. She didn't have much in common with her two stepsisters, Abundancia and Pulchritudina. Abundancia spent most of her free time making and managing her investment portfolio so that she could snag a wealthy husband, and Pulchritudina concentrated on making herself even more beautiful with fancy designer clothes and expensive makeovers. Ella spent what little free time she had either cultivating her mother's garden or curled up reading a book in the attic. She had a whole library to read left to her by her deceased mother. She read about knights of old and their fair ladies, about geography and travel, about politics and customs of foreign countries, about gardening, and about poetry. Simplyella read so much that she now had to wear reading glasses, but she didn't mind wearing glasses, even if her sisters made fun of them on her and told her she should be more concerned with how she looked. One day as she was reading a book on gardening, an envelope addressed to her fell out of the book she was reading.

ELLA: *(Enters)* It's a note from my dear mother! This note says:

> "I leave thee my most precious gift.
> The best for thee, my lovely child.
> These riches will last you all your life,
> So be a happy, well-read wife."

What a lovely note. I will treasure it always. *(Exits)*

NARRATOR: And Ella used the note as a bookmark for her place in the book she was reading on flowers. Now it happened that there was to be a big single's dance at the country club, and Abundancia and Pulchritudina went out to buy the most expensive and fancy dresses they could find. Ella realized that she would probably just have to read about the dance in the newspaper, since she did not have enough money to buy herself a new dress to wear. As she took out her note from her mother to read one more time, she noticed something else in the envelope. It was two twenty-dollar bills with a note clipped to them addressed to her from her mother. The note said she should use the money to purchase some material for a fine dress.

ELLA: *(Enters)* Thank you again, dear Mother. I will buy myself some beautiful material and design a new dress for the dance. *(Exits)*

NARRATOR: So Ella worked secretly on her dress. When she was finished sewing the dress, she realized that it was rather plain, but elegant nonetheless. After Abundancia and Pulchritudina went off to the dance in their foreign sports cars, Ella sneaked out of the house and walked to the dance by herself. At the dance, Abundancia and Pulchritudina immediately found dance partners. Abundancia found a stockbroker, while Pulchritudina caught the eye of a dress designer. No one seemed to notice Ella when she arrived at the dance.

ELLA: *(Enters)* Maybe I can just stay at the back of the dance floor and listen to the music and watch the others dancing.

NARRATOR: As she watched the dancers, she tapped her tiny feet to the music and hummed along. It wasn't long before a handsome young man asked Ella to dance.

MAN: *(Enters)* What is your name, young lady?

ELLA: Oh, I am called Simplyella. I am here just to watch my stepsisters as they dance. They do look lovely, don't they?

NARRATOR: And Ella pointed out the two girls to the man.

MAN: Those are two friends of mine that they are dancing with. Your sisters are wearing very expensive-looking dresses, but personally I prefer simple things—somehow the simple things are more elegant. I think your dress is very beautiful. Will you dance with me? *(The two dance)*

NARRATOR: And the man and Ella danced and talked through the whole night. When midnight struck, Ella realized that she had to leave because she had to walk home by herself before her sisters discovered her at the dance.

ELLA: I am sorry, sir, but I must go home. I have to be ready to do my early morning chores.

MAN: But when will I see you again?

ELLA: Later, I hope. I must leave now. Good-bye and thank you for a wonderful night. *(Exits)*

NARRATOR: And Ella raced off the dance floor, dropping her reading glasses from her purse. Her dance partner picked them up, however.

MAN: *(Pretend to pick up glasses)* I will see that girl again. She may be the girl I would like to marry.

(Man exits)

NARRATOR: The next day the men who danced with Abundancia and Pulchritudina came to the house to ask them both out again. Ella's dancing partner came with his two friends. In fact, he had been asking at every house if a young woman lived there who wore the glasses he had picked up. When he showed the glasses to the two stepsisters, they both looked at each other and exclaimed that those glasses certainly didn't belong to them. They didn't have to wear glasses, and they certainly didn't waste their time by reading. Ella heard them talking from the attic where she was reading.

ELLA: *(Enters)* Glasses? Oh, I wonder if someone found my reading glasses?

NARRATOR: And when Ella came downstairs in her old clothes, the young man handed her the lost glasses.

MAN: *(Enters)* It is a truly beautiful woman who doesn't need fancy clothes and makeup to be lovely. Let me introduce myself properly. My name is Jerome, and I am not as rich or successful as the two men your sisters danced with. I am a hardworking librarian. Would you consider going out with such a man of many interests but of moderate means?

ELLA: Oh, yes, I would be glad to go out with you.

NARRATOR: And Ella and Jerome dated and had many book discussions before they decided to get married. Ella never forgot her mother's words: "These riches will last you all your life. So be a happy, well-read wife."

JEROME: Are you ever sorry that you didn't marry the wealthy stockbroker that Abundancia married or the clothes designer that Pulchritudina married?

ELLA: I can truthfully say, dear Jerome, that I have got the richest husband of them all—for our riches will last us all of our lives.

The End

The Smallest Loaf of Bread

(a retelling of a German tale)

Puppets needed:

Man

Girl

Prop:

loaf of bread

NARRATOR: Once upon a time in the days of the Civil War there was a famine in some parts of the country. Families were going hungry, including the children. Now there was a rich old man who wanted to use his money to help the children by buying them food. He called all the neighborhood children to his home and bought as many loaves of bread as he could find—loaves of different sizes.

MAN: *(Enters)* I will give the children their choice of loaves of bread. *(Exits)*

NARRATOR: And the children came in and grabbed and gobbled up one large loaf after another, fighting each other for the biggest loaf of bread. In a few minutes, only one small child was left without any bread.

(Man and girl enter)

MAN: I am very sorry, young lady, but I have only one small loaf of bread left for you—the very smallest one.

GIRL: Oh, thank you, sir. This loaf will be just fine. It's big enough for me to share with my mother. Bless you for your kindness to all of us children. *(Exits with man)*

NARRATOR: When the girl got home and shared the loaf with her mother, out dropped several silver coins. The young girl had never seen such beautiful coins.

GIRL: *(Enters)* Oh, this good man has left these coins in the loaf by mistake. I must return the money to him so he can use the money to feed more children.

NARRATOR: And the girl went back to the rich man's home.

(Man enters)

GIRL: *(Calls out) Sir, sir!* Sir, I thank you for your generosity, but you made a big mistake. When I sliced open the loaf, these silver coins fell out. Surely you need these back.

MAN: My dear girl, that was no mistake. Come in, please. You did not grab for the largest loaf of bread like the other children. By taking the smallest loaf with gratitude and thanks, you proved your good nature. The coins are just an extra blessing just for you and your mother.

NARRATOR: And so, the little girl's good nature paid off handsomely—more handsomely than the other children's greed.

The End

Soup Made from a Nail

(a retelling of "Nail Soup")

Puppets needed:

Man
Woman

Props:

nail
pot

NARRATOR: Once upon a time there was an old man who couldn't find work. He wandered through the city and then into the countryside looking for a job, any job, that he could do to earn some money for food. Finally he found himself walking deep into the forest. It was getting dark, and he had to find a place to rest for the night and perhaps get a warm meal to eat. In the distance he saw a glimmer of light, and he walked over toward the light. It came from a small cottage. The man knocked softly on the cottage door.

MAN: *(Enters)* Hello. Anyone home?

WOMAN: *(Answering door, enters)* Who wants to know?

MAN: How do you do, madam? It is only I, an old man coming to seek a place to sleep and perhaps a meal. Could you help me?

WOMAN: I'm afraid I can't be bothered with company now. I've no food to feed myself, and you want me to feed you?

MAN: Perhaps you'd allow me to warm myself for a few minutes by the fire?

WOMAN: I suppose that would be OK as long as you don't stay long. I haven't eaten all day, and I'll probably get to bed soon.

MAN: Oh, certainly I will not stay long. Maybe just long enough to cook you a good meal.

WOMAN: You cook me a meal? With what?

MAN: Don't you worry. You just get me a cooking pot and I'll set to work. We'll both be eating in no time.

WOMAN: Well, here's the pot on the stove, but I can't imagine what you have to cook in it.

MAN: I have everything I need right in my pocket.

NARRATOR: And the man pulled out a nail from his pocket.

MAN:	Many a meal I have fixed with this nail, and many more meals I will use it for. It's a very special nail, you see.
WOMAN:	Looks like an ordinary nail to me.
MAN:	Let's start up the soup. First I put my nail in the pot of boiling water. Won't take long now. You wouldn't have a turnip or two to thicken the broth, would you?
WOMAN:	I think I have a couple of turnips in the pantry. *(Goes to check)* Here's a couple of turnips for the pot. *(Pretend to hand them to him)*
MAN:	That's great. This is going to taste so good. It would be even better if we had a little beef. You wouldn't have any leftover meat, would you?
WOMAN:	Let me check. I may have a little. *(Checks)* Here's some beef you can use. *(Pretend to hand him beef)*
MAN:	Great. I don't suppose you have any onions? One or two would make it even more flavorful.
WOMAN:	Sure. I can get you some onions for the pot. Here you go. *(Pretend to hand him onions)*
MAN:	How about a few carrots? Do you have any?
WOMAN:	I just picked a few from the garden. Here you are. *(Pretend to hand him carrots)*
MAN:	This is going to be the best soup you ever tasted, and it's almost ready to serve. Of course it would taste even better with a little salt and pepper. Bread and butter would go well with this too.
WOMAN:	I have some salt and pepper right here. What luck! I just baked bread this morning. We have plenty of bread to eat with the soup.
MAN:	Good. Let's sit down to eat.
WOMAN:	I can't wait to taste your soup. It smells so good.
MAN:	I just have to take out my special nail and we are ready to eat.
NARRATOR:	The old man and the woman both sat down to a wonderful feast. They both agreed that they had never had a better meal. When they were both full, they laughed and talked until it was time for bed.
MAN:	Thank you for a wonderful night. I'll go now.
WOMAN:	You'll do no such thing. There's an extra room for you to use for the night. You are most welcome to stay.

(Both exit)

NARRATOR:	So the old man rested comfortably that night. When he was ready to leave in the morning, the woman insisted that he take a loaf of fresh bread with him that she had just baked.

(Both enter)

MAN: How can I ever repay you for your kindness in befriending an old man like me?

WOMAN: Repay me? Why should you repay me for that delicious nail soup of yours? That was the best meal I have shared in a long while. Your company was good too.

MAN: Why, thank you, madam.

WOMAN: You know, if you are looking for a job, I think that you would make a great cook at the village inn. Everyone would like your special nail soup, and perhaps some nights you could come here to share some with me.

NARRATOR: And the old man found himself a home and a job at last—keeping the whole village fed on his nail soup.

WOMAN: To think, we owe it all to your special nail.

MAN: Not just the nail. Soup always tastes better when it's shared with a friend.

The End

The Stonecutter's Wish

(a retelling of a Japanese tale)

Puppet needed:

Stonecutter

Props:

rock (onstage)
robe

NARRATOR: Once upon a time many years ago in Japan lived a poor stonecutter who worked each day cutting stone from the side of a mountain. One day he saw a rich man pass by him on a fine horse. The rich man had beautiful clothes and many servants riding with him. The poor stonecutter looked at the rich man and was sad.

STONECUTTER: *(Enters)* Oh, if only I were as rich as that man, I could be happy. *(Exits)*

NARRATOR: A voice from the mountain on which he was working said, "You will have your wish." When the stonecutter returned home he found a rich palace instead of his humble hut. There were servants there to cater to his every need. Well, this life was amusing for a while, but soon the stonecutter became bored, since he had nothing useful to do all day long.

STONECUTTER: *(Enters)* The life of a rich man is not as interesting as I thought it would be. I should have wished for something else. Why didn't I wish to be a prince instead? I think I would be really happy if I were a prince. *(Exits)*

NARRATOR: And the voice from the mountain said, "You will have your wish. You will be a prince." So now the stonecutter became a prince. He was served the finest foods and rode in a fine golden carriage.

STONECUTTER: *(Enters with robe on)* This is truly the good life now. But I wish I could control the sun. I am a bit warm. I think I would be happier if I were the sun.

NARRATOR: And the voice from the mountain said, "You have your wish. You are now the sun."

STONECUTTER: But I wanted to be comfortable. Now I am always hot. No one wants to be around me anymore. I burn up everything and everyone I see. Oh, I wish I were a rain cloud. Then I could have some relief from the heat, and people would welcome me. *(Exits)*

NARRATOR: And the voice from the mountain said, "You are a rain cloud as you wish." And the stonecutter was happy for a while being a cloud. He was cooler, and the farmers welcomed his rain. However, one day the rains would not stop. Whole cities were flooding. Only the rocks remained safe from the waters.

STONECUTTER:

(Enters) Oh, I am no longer happy as a cloud now that the floods have started. I wish that I could be a rock on the mountainside. Those rocks are truly the most powerful force in the universe. They are not affected by the rains and floods.

NARRATOR: And the voice from the mountain said, "It is so. You are now a rock."

STONECUTTER:

(Sits on rock) Now at last no one is stronger than I—not the sun, not a prince, not a cloud. I am now the mightiest of all. But what is that tapping on my rock surface? Who is that man doing that? *(Make a tapping sound)*

NARRATOR: And the voice said, "Why that is a stonecutter—such as you were once."

STONECUTTER:

But he is mightier than the rock. He cuts through even the mighty boulders. If only I were that man again.

NARRATOR: And the voice from the mountain said, "It is so. You are now a stonecutter once again, just as you were." And never again did the poor stonecutter complain about his fate. He was happy and proud to be a humble stonecutter. Until the end of his life, the stonecutter never wished for anything else again.

The End

The Sun's Special Gift to Man

(a retelling of a Native American tale)

For a recent picture book version of this Cherokee legend, see Joseph Bruchac's *The First Strawberries* (New York: Dial, 1993).

Puppets needed:

    Native American man
    Native American woman

Props:

    basket of strawberries
    flowers (both optional)

NARRATOR: A Cherokee legend speaks of how Man was blessed with the sweet and delicious strawberry. In the beginning, the Great Spirit created the first man and woman as companions to each other. Now neither would have to live alone. For several years Man and Woman lived happily together as husband and wife, but this happiness did not last forever. One afternoon the man came home from the hunt and found that his wife was not home. He saw his wife in the meadow gathering flowers. His anger grew as he waited for her to return home. He was hungry and tired, after all, from a hard day's work. Finally the woman returned home laden with beautiful flowers.

(Man and Woman enter)

MAN: What is this? Why is my dinner not ready for me when I come home? You waste your time gathering flowers instead of making the dinner? I have been working all day long at the hunt, and you have nothing prepared for our meal. You have no time for gathering flowers. I am hungry. I want to eat!

NARRATOR: Now the woman was not used to her husband talking to her so harshly.

WOMAN: Do you not see that I have picked these flowers for you to look at and enjoy? I have not been wasting time. These flowers are food for the soul. They are truly beautiful, aren't they?

MAN: Beauty is one thing, and food is another. I need my dinner. I cannot eat beauty.

WOMAN: I have never heard you speak like this to me. If you cannot see the beauty in flowers, I can no longer stay with you. I will leave you now. Do not bother to follow me. *(Exits)*

NARRATOR:	The husband tried to stop his wife from leaving, but he could not. He saw that she was determined to leave him. All he could do was to try to follow her and convince her to come home. But she was so swift. Try as he might, he knew he could never catch her without help. Now luckily for Man, the Great Spirit was watching from above. He saw and heard the quarrel between the man and the woman. When Man asked for help from above, the Spirit sent his powerful Sun to help the unhappy man.
MAN:	I was wrong to speak so harshly to my beloved wife. I must go after her and try to get her to come home. (*Exits*)
NARRATOR:	(*Woman enters*) Sun tried to help by sending his rays down on the earth so that lovely red raspberries would grow in the woman's path. Sun hoped that the woman would stop and taste the berries. Then her husband might be able to catch up to her.
WOMAN:	(*Walks on*) I see those pretty red berries in my path, but I will not stop to pick them now. I must be on my way.
NARRATOR:	So Sun tried a second time. He poured his rays down on the earth even more brightly so that another berry could grow. This time a blueberry bush sprang up in her path, filled with plump blueberries. Maybe these berries would tempt the woman to stop and eat.
WOMAN:	What lovely blueberries in my path, but I must not stop to eat. I have to travel further. I do not want my husband to find me.
NARRATOR:	So Sun tried one last time. With all his might, Sun poured his rays on the earth and produced a third kind of berry, even more lovely to look at. This berry was a beautiful red color. The berries looked like large red jewels. They were the first strawberries.
WOMAN:	These berries I cannot resist. I must stop and pick some. (*Tries one*) Why, these are delicious to eat. I wonder if my husband would enjoy some of these lovely berries for his dinner? Perhaps I can pick some and bring them home for both of us to eat and enjoy.
MAN:	(*Enters*) Wife, thank goodness I have found you. Please forgive me for the way I spoke to you. Can you forget my unkindness and come home?
WOMAN:	I do forgive you. To prove that I forgive you, I have a special gift for you to try. Try some of these beautiful ripe berries I have gathered for our dinner. What good are such great gifts from the Creator if we cannot share them?
MAN:	Thank you, my wife. You have taught me to eat my words, my dear.
WOMAN:	What do you mean, Husband?

MAN: I told you that I could not eat beauty, but you have shown me how to do just that. From this time on, these lovely berries will remind me to be good and sweet to you—as sweet as these lovely red berries.

NARRATOR: And the man and the woman continued to laugh together and to pop the delicious red berries into each other's mouth. The Great Spirit saw that Sun had done well. He bade him return each spring to shine down on the strawberry plants. So every year, even today, the Cherokee people anxiously await Sun's golden rays on their strawberry harvest, for these sweet fruits remain a gift from the Great Spirit to man. They are a reminder that all men and women should take time to appreciate and share the bounty and goodness of nature as well as that all men and women should be kind and good to each other with a love as sweet and renewing as the juice of the luscious red strawberry.

The End

The Troll's Toll Bridge

(a retelling of "The Three Billy Goats Gruff")

Puppets needed:

Troll

Little Billy Goat

Prop:

bridge (leave onstage)

NARRATOR: Once upon a time there was a young troll who lived under a wooden bridge. He had moved there recently after the previous troll occupant under the bridge had met with a terrible accident. Troll Realty would never say more about the incident than that there was an unfortunate misunderstanding between the troll and a local Big Billy Goat Gruff. That's all the Realtor would say, other than the accommodations under the bridge were available quite reasonably. The young troll was settling in well, but he was getting a bit lonesome since so few ever crossed the bridge above his home. Troll couldn't figure out why there was so little traffic over the bridge. Now word had gotten out in the neighborhood that trolls were mean—very mean—and that they had huge appetites. All the animals avoided that bridge and took the long way around the water, especially after the Big Billy Goat Gruff incident. One day a brave little goat started to cross the bridge. He had decided to see this new troll for himself. "Trip, trap, trip, trap," went his hooves on the wooden bridge above the troll's head, waking him up in the morning.

(Troll—under the bridge—and Goat enter)

TROLL: Who's that tripping across my bridge?

GOAT: It's only I, a young Billy Goat Gruff come to cross the bridge to get to the green pasture on the other side. Please don't eat me.

TROLL: Eat you? What makes you think I want to eat you?

GOAT: Well, that's what the former occupant threatened to do when my cousins tried to cross the bridge a few months ago.

TROLL: He did? If you want to cross my bridge, you are going to have to tell me the whole story of the troll and Big Billy Goat Gruff. I think that is a fair exchange for your using my bridge.

NARRATOR: But Little Billy Goat Gruff was afraid of telling the story about the old troll. What if the young troll took it the wrong way and got mad? The goat decided that he would stretch out the story of the troll, leaving off at a good point so that the troll would let him cross the bridge several times.

GOAT: You see it happened like this. I had some Gruff cousins older than I. They were called the Three Billy Goats Gruff, because the three of them always hung around together. When spring came, they longed to eat the sweet grass that grows on the other side of the mountain, but to get the grass, they had to cross this old wooden bridge. Now a mean old troll, no offense to present company, lived under the bridge—a troll who liked to eat goats. Need I say more?

TROLL: Yes, please go on. This is getting interesting.

GOAT: I'd love to go on, but I am starving. How about if I catch you after I've eaten a little of the grass on the other side? Then I'll continue my story.

TROLL: Well, if you promise. OK. Hurry along and eat. I'll be waiting.

(Goat exits)

NARRATOR: And Little Billy Goat scampered over the bridge. "Trip, trap, trip, trap." Soon all the troll could hear was the tinkling in the distance of the little bell that the goat wore around his neck. Later in the day, the troll heard the bell more clearly as well as the trip, trap of his hooves once again on the bridge.

TROLL: Who's that tripping across my bridge?

(Goat enters)

GOAT: It's only I, Little Billy Goat Gruff, come to tell you more of that story.

TROLL: Good. Please do. I've been waiting for you to come back.

GOAT: Well, after the old troll said his line, "Who is that tripping across my bridge," my little cousin Billy Goat told the old troll that he was too young and small a goat to be a good meal. He convinced the troll to wait to eat his older brother, who would be coming across the bridge soon.

TROLL: Makes sense. So what happened next? Go on.

GOAT: *(Yawns)* You know, I could probably tell this story better after a good night's sleep. How about if I come back tomorrow to tell you more?

TROLL: *(Yawns)* OK. To tell the truth, I am a bit tired too. See you tomorrow then. Don't forget.

(Goat exits)

NARRATOR: And the Little Billy Goat scampered home. The next morning he trotted back to the bridge and tried to cross quietly before the troll woke up. "Trip, trap, trip, trap." His hooves sounded on the wooden bridge. No such luck, though. The troll heard the goat and rushed outside.

TROLL:	Who's that trotting across my bridge?
GOAT:	It's only I, Little Billy Goat Gruff, who is going over the bridge to eat more grass on the other side.
TROLL:	Oh, no you are not. Not so fast. Have you forgotten?
GOAT:	Forgotten that you are going to eat me?
TROLL:	No, silly, forgotten that you were going to continue that story. We got to the part that the small Billy Goat had convinced the troll he was too little to eat. He told the troll to wait for his older second brother.
GOAT:	Oh, yes, well pretty soon the second Billy Goat Gruff came across the bridge. "Who's that clomping across my bridge?" yelled the troll. "It's only I, the second Billy Goat Gruff come to eat some grass on the other side of the bridge. You don't want to waste your time with a goat like me and ruin your appetite for my brother who is coming after me. Do you?" The old troll told him to be off. The second goat scampered across the bridge to eat in the fine pasture.
TROLL:	So far, this story isn't too exciting, Little Goat. When do we get to the good part?
GOAT:	Soon, but I have to eat my breakfast first. Catch you on the way back.

(Goat exits)

NARRATOR:	And the troll settled in under the bridge waiting for the goat to return. Soon he heard the tripping of goat hooves on the bridge.

(Goat enters)

TROLL:	Who's that tromping on my bridge?
GOAT:	It's only I, Little Billy Goat Gruff. Want to hear some more of the story?
TROLL:	Sure, but make it quick this time.
GOAT:	Why? So you can eat me up?
TROLL:	No, so I can get to bed. I've had a busy day.
GOAT:	Well, soon Big Billy Goat Gruff came by. He was the biggest and strongest of the goats. When he stomped across the bridge he made a terribly loud noise. "Who's that stomping across my bridge?" said the old troll. "It's I, the biggest and strongest Billy Goat Gruff. I'm going to the other side to eat the fine grass that grows there." "Oh, no you are not," said the troll. "I let your two brothers go, but now I'm going to eat you. You'll make a fine feast."
TROLL:	This is getting good. What happened next?
GOAT:	Well, to tell the truth, I'm getting a little too tired to remember the ending. I'll tell it to you tomorrow.

NARRATOR: Little Billy Goat scampered home for a good night's rest. He tossed and turned, however, all night. How was he going to tell the ending of the story without making the troll mad? The next day he lightly tripped over the bridge. "Trip, trap, trip, trap."

(Goat enters)

TROLL: Who's that tripping over my bridge? Is it you, Little Billy Goat, coming for breakfast?

GOAT: Oh, no. Don't eat me for breakfast.

TROLL: Eat you? What I meant was, do you want some breakfast while you finish telling me the end of the story?

GOAT: OK. Well, the oldest Billy Goat Gruff lowered his head and on either side of his head were terrible, sharp, big horns. He rushed toward the mean old troll and butted him as hard as he could, throwing the troll in the water. The old troll was never heard from again.

TROLL: *(Sniffing)* That was such a good story. Never heard from again, huh? Poor old troll.

GOAT: Are you mad at me now? Are you going to eat me?

TROLL: Why should I be mad at you? I guess it all goes to show how important it is to share—to be a friendly neighbor. Do you think there are other animals around here that might want to use the bridge but are afraid of me?

GOAT: Well, you are a troll, aren't you?

TROLL: Don't judge every troll by that last one. From now on I'm going to allow everyone to cross the bridge, but it won't be free.

GOAT: You are going to charge a high toll?

TROLL: Yes, a toll. Everyone who wants to cross my bridge has to greet me before crossing and tell me a story on the way back.

GOAT: That's all? A story? You aren't going to eat them?

TROLL: Heavens, no. I'm a vegetarian. I have the loveliest mushroom garden under the bridge that keeps me fed all year-round.

(Both exit)

NARRATOR: And so Little Goat trotted happily home and told all his friends and neighbors that a new troll was in town. This troll only wanted friends, not meals. To help the troll notice when guests were using the bridge, Little Billy Goat left him his neck bell to hang on the door. All the troll's guests now rang the bell before crossing the bridge. With all the bridge traffic, the troll made more friends and heard more stories that he could have ever imagined. It was the stories that Little Billy Goat Gruff told, however, that he liked best. The troll would call out.

TROLL: *(Enters)* Who's that tripping across my bridge?

NARRATOR: And Little Billy Goat would say,

GOAT: *(Enters)* It's only I, Little Billy Goat Gruff. Are you going to eat me?

NARRATOR: And they both would break out laughing.

(Both laugh)

The End

Why Bear Has a Short Tail

(a retelling of a *pourquoi* tale)

Puppets needed:

Bear
Fox

Prop:

string of fish (optional)

NARRATOR: Once upon a time Bear had a nice, long furry tail. Why, his tail was even longer and furrier than Fox's. Fox was jealous of Bear's tail and was always comparing his tail with Bear's. One day, Fox met Bear in the woods. Fox had just stolen a whole line of fish, and he was carrying them back to his den.

(Fox, with fish, and Bear enter)

BEAR: Fox, what wonderful looking fish! How did you catch them? Do you have a special pole you use? You must be quite a fisherman. Maybe you can give me some pointers on fishing.

NARRATOR: Sly Fox wanted Bear to believe he had caught the fish himself and not stolen them. He also thought that he had a good chance to play a trick on Bear.

FOX: Yes, these are fine fish, aren't they? I catch this many every day. You could too if you would follow my fishing advice. Would you like to try?

BEAR: Sure. What would I have to do?

FOX: Just follow my instructions exactly. You see, I don't use a fishing pole.

BEAR: You don't?

FOX: No, I use my beautiful long tail to fish.

BEAR: Well, I could use my tail. It's even longer than yours, after all.

FOX: I suppose you could. What you have to do is cut a large hole in the ice and dangle your tail in the hole. The fish won't be able to resist biting your tail. That's how you catch them. Now, when you feel a sting in your tail, that means a fish is biting. You'll have to put up with a little pain in order to catch a number of fish. Leave your tail in that hole as long as you can so you'll have a lot of fish. When your tail feels like it is full of fish, then pull your tail out of the hole as quickly and hard as you can. Think you can do all that?

BEAR: I think so, Fox. Thanks for telling me about your new method of fishing. I surely love fresh fish.

FOX: See you later, Bear. Good luck to you now.

                        (Bear and Fox exit)

NARRATOR: And Bear hurried to the river to cut a hole in the ice. After a few minutes, he got very cold—especially his tail.

                        (Bear enters)

BEAR: Gee, I guess I'm doing this the right way, because I do feel my tail stinging. Fish must be biting my tail like crazy. I'll leave it in the hole for a few more minutes.

NARRATOR: When Bear couldn't stand it a second longer, he thought it was time to pull his tail out of the hole.

BEAR: I've got to do this quickly now as Fox said. Gee, I'm trying to stand up, but I can't budge. Why, I think the ice has got my tail frozen stuck. Well, here goes. I'll pull up my tail quickly and hard. *(Pulls)* Owwwww! *(Bear exits)*

NARRATOR: Well, Bear's tail did come out, but only a stub of his tail. Most of his long beautiful tail was left in that ice hole. Poor Bear had lost his tail and didn't have any fish to eat either. Bear slunk home with his little tail between his legs. As for Fox, he tried to stay out of Bear's way for a few days. In fact, Bear is still mad about his stubby tail, so if you ever see him, don't ever mention his tail. Ever since he lost his tail, Bear has hardly spoken to Fox. And Fox, by the way, always puts his tail between his legs when he meets Bear. He doesn't want to bring up a sensitive subject, after all. That Fox is no fool.

                        The End

The Wolf and Granny's Lost Glasses

(a retelling of "Little Red Riding Hood")

Puppets needed:
Wolf
Granny

Props:
red cloak
basket

NARRATOR: Once upon a time Wolf was sick of watching Little Red Riding Hood take all the goodies she made to her Granny. And he was just as sick and tired of seeing Little Red skipping home with her basket filled with freshly baked cookies she had gotten from her Granny.

WOLF: *(Enters)* Must be nice to have a Granny to make all those delicious cookies. I don't have a Granny to bake for me. I think I'll just pull a little switch and pretend I'm Little Red Riding Hood. Maybe Granny will give me some of her freshly baked cookies. *(Exits)*

NARRATOR: So Wolf got himself a red cloak and a basket for goodies and set off for Red Riding Hood's Granny's house. On the way, he made up some mud pies with ooey, gooey mud so that it would look like he was bringing treats for Granny. Now what Wolf didn't know was that Granny had misplaced her glasses this morning before she did her daily baking. When she was reaching for the sugar to add to the cookie dough, she grabbed the salt instead.

WOLF: *(Enters in red cloak)* I'll just knock on Granny's door and see if she thinks I'm Little Red Riding Hood. I'll leave my hood on just in case. *(Knocks)*

GRANNY: *(Enters)* Coming. Oh, I'll bet it's Little Red coming to visit. She loves my cookies. Who is it?

WOLF: It's Little Red, Granny. I've come to see you, and I've brought you some pies I just baked.

GRANNY: Just a minute, dear. *(Goes to door)* Come in, sweetie. Poor old Granny has lost her glasses this morning, so it takes me a while to get around. Come sit at the table with me. My cookies are still in the oven, but they are almost done. We can enjoy them in a few minutes.

NARRATOR: Wolf's mouth was watering at the sound of warm cookies fresh out of the oven.

WOLF: What kind of cookies did you fix today, Granny?

GRANNY: Why they are your favorite, dear—sugar cookies—made with a little extra sugar, just as you like them.

WOLF: Yum. Yum. I could gobble them all up. I mean, I can't wait for the cookies.

GRANNY: It won't be long, dear. How about opening up your basket and taking a taste of that pie you brought to tide you over until the cookies are baked?

WOLF: No, Granny. This pie is for you to enjoy later. I couldn't eat one now.

GRANNY: I insist, dear. I had a big breakfast earlier, and I am not in the least hungry yet. You just enjoy a few bites of that pie you brought.

WOLF: Well . . . (Takes a bite and chokes)

NARRATOR: And Wolf ate a few bites of the mud pies he brought. They were pretty disgusting, but he managed to choke down a few bites. After all, he'd get to eat all the sugar cookies in just a few minutes.

GRANNY: There now. That's better. Now you won't be so hungry for those cookies. Let Granny look at you, Little Red. I know that Granny can't see too well without her glasses, but you have really grown lately. What big teeth you have!

WOLF: The better to eat all those cookies. I mean, taste those cookies with, Granny.

GRANNY: And Little Red, what a big nose you have! You must take after your father's side of the family.

WOLF: The better to smell those cookies before I gobble them all up. I mean, I love the smell of freshly baked cookies.

GRANNY: Such a dear girl! And what lovely big brown eyes you have!

WOLF: The better to see those cookies with, Granny, as they all pop into my mouth. I mean, the better to see, so I can take the cookies out of the oven for you, Granny.

GRANNY: You are such a thoughtful grandchild. I'm so lucky. I think that the cookies are just about done. Will you help me put them on the table so that we can eat them?

WOLF: Gladly, Granny.

NARRATOR: And Wolf reached inside the oven to grab the sheets of cookies. He should have worn an oven mitt, but he was so anxious for those cookies, he didn't take the time to put a mitt on. So, he burned his paw.

WOLF: Oh, ow!

GRANNY: What is it, dear?

WOLF: It's nothing, Granny. *(Pours cookies into mouth)*

NARRATOR: And Wolf emptied all the hot cookies into his large mouth all at once. Suddenly he started to choke and then to moan as he closed his mouth around the salty cookies. They were the worst he ever tasted—even worse than the mud pies he had brought. Wolf ran out of Granny's house, never to be seen in the neighborhood again. He managed a muffled good-bye.

WOLF: *(Mouth stuffed with cookies)* Good-bye! Good riddance! That Granny is the worst cook I have ever seen in my life. Poor Little Red! *(Exits)*

NARRATOR: And Granny? Well, she did wonder why Little Red left the house so quickly.

GRANNY: That's kids for you. Such a sweet girl, though, and how she has grown! Lucky I made all those cookies for her. She does have a big appetite all right.

The End

Wolfi and the Three Squealers

(a retelling of "The Three Little Pigs")

Puppets needed:

Wolfi

Father Wolf

Pig

Props:

NARRATOR: Once upon a time there was a wolf called Wolfgang. He had been named after the great composer Mozart because he, like Mozart, had great musical ability and was precocious, or musically gifted at a young age, ever since he was a cub, in fact. Wolfgang, or Wolfi, as he was affectionately called by his parents, was the son of Luciano, the singing wolf, and Margot, a wolf known for her grace and dancing ability. Luciano, his father, taught Wolfi how to sing. He showed Wolfi how to practice breath control and how to project his voice. His mother taught Wolfi to move gracefully—the better to sneak up quietly on his prey. One day Wolfi was practicing his lessons in voice control so he could huff and puff better.

(Wolfi and Father Wolf enter)

FATHER WOLF:

You have to learn to huff and puff well. It's expected of you. It's what we wolves do. I know that I have taught you to sing well. All that practice with breath control will help you with your huffs and puffs. Singing is certainly good and enjoyable, but when you are an adult wolf, you have to make a good living—bring home the bacon, so to speak. I'd like you to practice on the home of that little pig down the road. The home doesn't appear to be built very well. I think a few good huffs and puffs should do it. You go there and huff and puff your best, and blow the house in. Then bring that pig home to us. I think you are ready, Wolfi. Want to try?

WOLFI: To tell the truth, Dad, I think I should practice my breath control a little more. My huffs are not very loud.

FATHER WOLF:

Nonsense. Go off with you. You'll be just fine. *(Father Wolf exits)*

NARRATOR: Well, Wolfi got to the house of the little pig and stood outside for a minute softly rehearsing.

WOLFI   (*Softly*) Little pig, little pig, let me come in or I'll huff and I'll puff and I'll blow your house in.

NARRATOR: As he was practicing, he heard the voices of three little pigs inside, and they were singing "Row, Row, Row Your Boat" in high-pitched little squeals. Suddenly he found himself singing along in his nice lower-pitched voice.

WOLFI: (*Sings*) Row, row, row your boat, gently down the stream . . .

NARRATOR: Soon one of the pigs came to the door.

PIG: (*Enters*) Will you listen to that? What a lovely voice you have.

WOLFI: I'll huff and I'll puff . . .

PIG: No need for that. You can practice later. Come on in and join our musical group. We need a lower voice. (*Calls inside*) Oh, pigs, guess what we've got? A nice tenor voice at last for our group.

(Pig and Wolfi exit)

NARRATOR: Well, Wolfi wasn't prepared for this response, but he did have a good time singing with the pigs. When he got home and Dad asked where the bacon was, Wolfi just shrugged his shoulders. This time Mother Wolf stepped in and showed Wolfi some new dance steps so he could gracefully creep up on the pigs and surprise them next time.

(Wolfi enters)

WOLFI: I'll try again, and this time I'll be quieter so I can say my full huff-and-puff speech.

NARRATOR: And Wolfi went again to the little pig's house. This time he crept up gracefully and quietly and did a few dance steps before knocking.

WOLFI: (*Creeps gracefully*) Little pig, little pig, let me come in, or I'll huff and I'll puff and I'll . . .

PIG: (*Enters*) Oh, great. It's you again, Wolfi. Come on in. I saw those dance steps you did though the window. Can you teach us pigs how to move gracefully like you do? I just love those new dance moves.

(Pig and Wolfi exit)

NARRATOR: And so Wolfi spent some time coaching the pigs on their dance steps. He came home empty-handed—no huffing and puffing and no pig. Finally Father Wolf told Wolfi to try one more time. "Third time's a charm," said Father Wolf. So Wolfi marched up to the pig's house and let out his prepared speech in his loudest voice.

WOLFI: (*Enters*) Little pig, little pig, let me come in, or I'll huff and I'll puff and I'll blow your house in. (*Huffs and puffs*)

PIG: *(Enters)* Oh, Wolfi, it's you. Come on in. You surely speak loudly. I'll bet you can huff and puff with the best of them. That was the most masterful bit of huffing and puffing that I have heard in a long time. Have you ever considered playing a tuba? Such breath control. Just what we need to accompany us in our musical number. Want to join our musical act?

WOLFI: Why, I guess so, little pig. I should ask my folks, though.

(Wolfi and Pig exit)

NARRATOR: So Wolfi went home and explained about his new job to his dad.

(Wolfi and Father Wolf enter)

WOLFI: You know what you said about huffing and puffing, Dad?

FATHER WOLF:

Yes, Son.

WOLFI: Well, I discovered that I'm not much good at blowing down a house, but I have a good enough voice to be a part of a new musical act called Wolfi and the Three Squealers. If it hadn't been for you and Mom with all your advice and help, I would never have been asked to do this. What do you think, Dad?

FATHER WOLF:

Well, Son, that is not exactly the career your mother and I had in mind for you, but I know you do have great musical talent. Invite those little pigs in for dinner some time. This time we'll feed them and not eat them. After all, you will still be bringing home the bacon.

The End

The Woman Who Refused to Share

(a retelling of a *pourquoi* tale)

Puppets needed:

Man
Old woman
Bird (woodpecker)

Props:

NARRATOR: Once upon a time there was a prosperous old widow who had lived alone for so long she had grown very selfish. One day she had decided to bake something special just for herself.

WOMAN: *(Enters)* I think I would enjoy eating some of my favorite cakes for dinner. I can prepare several cakes and eat them all myself. I'll put on a clean apron and my little red cap on my head while I cook. First I'll take out the sugar, eggs, milk, flour, and raisins. I'll mix up a fine dough. Then I will pour it out and bake it up in the oven. I can't wait to taste my cakes. They surely smell good while they are baking.

NARRATOR: As the woman was about to take the cakes out of the oven, a poor old man was passing by her window and smelled the cakes baking. They smelled so good, and he was very hungry.

MAN: *(Enters)* Madam, would you let me have just a few bites of one of your cakes to eat? I haven't eaten anything all day. Could you spare me just a little cake? I'll be glad to do a chore for you or stay around and keep you company for awhile.

WOMAN: Oh, I don't think so. I don't need any company. You see all these cakes are for me to eat. I suppose I could bake you a small cake after I enjoy my own cake. You can just wait outside while I eat my cake.

NARRATOR: So the old man waited outside, whistling a song while he waited. After she had eaten her fill of the cake, the woman twisted off a small piece of dough and patted it into a tiny cake. Right before her eyes, though, the tiny piece of dough started growing bigger and bigger until it became a nice large cake.

WOMAN: I'm very sorry, but I won't be able to give you this cake. It's too nice and large to give away. I'll save this one for later for myself and fix you a smaller one. Just wait outside for a bit longer.

NARRATOR: The old woman pinched off another small piece of dough from the bowl. This piece was much smaller than before, but once again, when

114   The Woman Who Refused to Share

she placed it in the baking pan, the dough filled up the pan and became a good-sized cake.

WOMAN: Will you look at that lovely, large cake. Well, I'm sorry, old man, but I couldn't possibly give you this cake either. It came out perfectly. I'll save it for tomorrow's meal. Please be off with you now, I'd like to eat my meal in peace. *(Man and woman exit)*

NARRATOR: And the woman finished off all of her cakes by herself. As she was eating the last bites, though, she noticed something happening to her. She was changing: her mouth was turning into a beak, her head and hands were growing feathers, and her feet were changing into claws.

BIRD: *(Enters)* Oh, no, I've turned into a bird! Now how am I going to be able to finish all my cakes? For that matter, how am I ever going to make myself more cakes?

NARRATOR: Yes, the selfish old woman had become a bird. You might still hear her today hopping up and down on the trees searching for food. She is always hungry now. She has to peck, peck, peck to find something to eat. You see, she turned into a woodpecker. So if you hear that tap, tap, tapping on a tree, it may be the old woman. Don't expect her to be friendly or to sing you a pretty song. She's just too hungry, and she's too worried about finding her next meal to sing a song for anyone.

The End

Zucchini Bread

(a retelling of "The Little Red Hen")

Puppets needed:
Little Red Hen
Chick

Prop:
bowl (optional)

NARRATOR: Remember the tale of the Little Red Hen and the cake she made without the help of her roommates the cat, the dog, and the mouse? Well, this is a story that takes place several months later. Little Red Hen is now a mother hen who lives with her little chicks. One evening one of the little chicks who was especially interested in cooking and in eating was pecking through Little Red Hen's recipe book. She came to Little Red Hen with a question.

(Little Red Hen and Chick enter)

CHICK: Mama, how do you pronounce this word in my book? It's spelled Z-u-c-c-h-i-n-i?

MAMA: That's my recipe for zucchini bread, dear.

CHICK: Zucchini. I like the sound of that word.

NARRATOR: And little chick ran around singing, "Zuk-ee-ne, zuk-eye-ne. You spell it with an 'i-ni.'"

CHICK: Do you think I would like this zucchini bread, Mama?

MAMA: I think so, dear. It's a lot of work to make, though.

CHICK: Mama, won't you make zucchini bread? I love the name, and I want to try it. Please, Mama, please bake it up right now.

MAMA: Little Chick, to make zucchini bread, we need to grow some zucchini squash and add lots of other ingredients. Will you be willing to help me get everything ready to make it, Little Chick?

CHICK: Oh, yes, Mama. I'll help.

MAMA: First we have to plant some zucchini squash seeds. Then we must weed the baby plants and water them so that they will grow big and plump.

NARRATOR: And Little Chick was so excited, she started to make up a song.

CHICK: *(Sings)*

First we plant zucchini seeds.
Then we have to watch them grow.

Then we have to pull the weeds.
All for our zucchini bread.

(*Both exit*)

NARRATOR: And Little Chick and Mama worked together in the garden planting and weeding and watering the zucchini.

(*Both enter*)

CHICK: Oh, Mama, the zucchini plants are growing very big. Can we pick them soon?

MAMA: We have to wait a few more days, Little Chick, but meantime you need to weed and water some more.

CHICK: I will, Mama.

(*Both exit*)

NARRATOR: And so, Little Red Hen and her chick worked on the garden and soon were able to pick a whole bushel basket of zucchini squash.

(*Both enter*)

CHICK: What other ingredients do we need to gather together, Mama?

MAMA: We need three fresh eggs, some vegetable oil, some brown sugar and some granulated sugar, vanilla, flour, baking soda, cinnamon, salt, and nuts. Then we have to grate some of our zucchini. We have to do the grating very carefully.

CHICK: I'll help to get all the ingredients gathered and to grate the zucchini. I'll be very careful doing the grating, Mama.

(*Both exit*)

NARRATOR: And Little Chick and her Mama worked together to gather the ingredients they needed. Little Chick sang as she worked.

(*Both enter*)

CHICK: (*Sings*) Zuk-ee-ne, zuk-eye-ne. You spell it with an "i-ni." Now what, Mama?

MAMA: Will you help me mix all the ingredients together and sift in the flour?

CHICK: I surely will, Mama.

NARRATOR: And Little Chick and her mama mixed all the ingredients well and poured the dough into two large loaf pans.

CHICK: (*Sings*)

Then we sift the flour in.
Mix in all the other stuff.
Then we pour it in the pans.
All for our zucchini bread.

Are we ready to bake the bread, Mama?

MAMA: Yes, dear. We bake it for an hour or so. Set the timer in the kitchen, Little Chick.

CHICK: I will, Mama.

(Both exit)

NARRATOR: And Little Red Hen and her chick waited for a whole hour while the bread baked. Chick was getting impatient.

(Both enter)

CHICK: It sure smells good, Mama. I'm getting awfully hungry.

MAMA: After it is baked, we need to let the bread cool for half an hour. Can you be patient and wait, Little Chick?

CHICK: I can, Mama, but it'll be hard. *(Sings)*

> Then we bake zucchini bread.
> We will wait for it to cool.
> It smells very, very good.
> Mama's great zucchini bread.

NARRATOR: After the bread cooled, it was ready to eat.

CHICK: The bread looks wonderful, Mama. Thank you so much for making this zucchini bread. Can we eat some of your bread now, Mama?

MAMA: I'm afraid it's not my zucchini bread. You helped me plant the zucchini. You helped me water and weed the plants. You helped me pick the zucchini squash. You helped me gather all the ingredients together and mix the dough. You helped me pour it into the pans and to bake it. Now who do you think gets to eat this zucchini bread?

CHICK: Can't I get a small piece of your bread, Mama?

MAMA: I don't think so, Little Chick. You see, it's not my bread, as I was telling you. It's our bread.

NARRATOR: And so Little Red Hen and her little chick sat down and shared the zucchini bread. Together they ate every single delicious bite. And any time Little Red Hen asked for help baking any bread or cake, guess who was always willing to help? You guessed it.

CHICK: *(Sings)*

> After we have grown our squash,
> After we have made the dough,
> After we have baked it up,
> We can eat zucchini bread.
> Yum, yum!

The End

Androcles and the Lion

Puppets needed:
    Androcles, the slave
    Lion

Props:
    none

NARRATOR: One upon a time, long, long ago in ancient Roman times, there was a slave called Androcles. He had been a slave for many years, working hard in the fields for a cruel Roman master. Recently he thought of a way to escape from his slavery. He would go off into the forest and disappear.

ANDROCLES: *(Enters)* I think if I am careful about getting away close to nighttime, it will be difficult for the master to find me. I should be safe if I move very quickly and don't stop anywhere for a long rest.

NARRATOR: But just as he was on his way through the forest, he heard a pitiful moaning and groaning sound coming from some animal ahead of him in the forest. *(Lion moans and groans backstage)*

ANDROCLES: I probably should turn this other way in order to avoid being attacked by that animal. It sounds like it is wounded. If I help the animal, I might get caught and brought back to the master. *(Lion moans again)* Oh, whatever animal is making that sound is in a great deal of pain. I can't just let it suffer so.

NARRATOR: So Androcles went in the direction of the moaning and found a lion lying down on the ground in great pain. *(Lion enters from other side)*

ANDROCLES: Unarmed as I am, I am no match for a wild lion. He could eat me alive if I approach too near him.

NARRATOR: But as Androcles came near, the lion just held up one of his paws, which was swollen and red. Androcles could see what was wrong. *(Lion holds up one paw)*

ANDROCLES: Oh, I see what it is. There is a large thorn that has worked into that sore paw and is causing you such agony, friend Lion. If you will allow me to do so, I think I can help you. You must trust me not to hurt you.

NARRATOR:	Androcles looked deeply into the lion's eyes. (*Androcles looks at Lion*)
ANDROCLES:	There now. I think if you will hold still, I can pull this thorn out. (*He yanks on the thorn*) Now I must just bandage up this wound so it can heal. I will use a piece of my garment. (*Pretend to tear garment and bandage the wound*)
NARRATOR:	As Androcles finished with the lion's paw, the lion put his head down and licked the hand of Androcles in gratitude and friendship.
ANDROCLES:	You are most welcome, friend Lion, but where am I to hide now that darkness has come? (*Both exit*)
NARRATOR:	As if he understood, the lion led Androcles to his cave. Once it was morning, the lion bounded out of the cave to search for meat to feed himself and Androcles, his new friend. Both the lion and Androcles were able to survive like this for several days, until a search party captured both Androcles and the lion. Both would be used in the Colosseum. After Androcles was returned to his master, his punishment was that he would be thrown to the lions. The emperor and his court came to view this spectacle. Androcles was made to walk forward into the arena to meet his death at the mercy of a vicious lion.
ANDROCLES:	(*Enters*) I will go forth with dignity. I will not cry or be afraid. I will only pray for a swift death.
NARRATOR:	He heard mighty roars from the stadium, for the lions had not been fed in a few days so that they would be more hungry and vicious. (*Lion roars*) Androcles bravely went into the stadium. (*Lion enters*) But when Androcles approached the lion, instead of rushing out to pounce on him, the lion suddenly stopped, sniffed Androcles, licked his hand, and settled at his feet.
ANDROCLES:	It is my friend, my own lion friend! Hello, dear Lion.
NARRATOR:	And Androcles walked with the lion around the arena, as if the lion were his pet. The crowds cheered their approval. (*Crowds scream, "Hurrah!"*) The emperor freed both Androcles and the lion, because the spectacle he had witnessed was the most surprising and exciting one he had ever seen. And Androcles and the lion were allowed to live in the forest in a cabin for the rest of their days. One moral of this story is that no kind deed we do goes unrewarded. You might also say that sometimes by helping someone else, we can save ourselves.

The End

The Boy Who Cried "Wolf"

Puppets needed:

   Shepherd boy
   Wolf

Props:

NARRATOR: Once upon a time there was a lazy shepherd boy who grew very tired of the job his father gave him to do. Every day the boy had to take the family's flock of sheep to the nearby meadow and guard them while they grazed. The job was not difficult, but it was very boring. The boy had no one to talk to and little to do for hours every day. After a few weeks, he couldn't stand the quiet one more minute.

SHEPHERD: *(Enters)* Father says that I have to stay here all day, and there's absolutely nothing for me to do all day long. How can I put a little bit of excitement in this awful job? I don't think I can stand this all summer long by myself.

NARRATOR: After a while of thinking about it, the boy came up with a plan.

SHEPHERD: I know what I can do. I can get the people in town to come to the meadow if I pretend that a wolf is after the flock. I just have to call out an alarm. That will get their attention. I think I'll try it right now. Here goes. *(Yells)* Wolf! Wolf! Help! A wolf is attacking our sheep! *(Exits)*

NARRATOR: It didn't take very long for the people of the village to hear the cries and come to the aid of the sheep and the shepherd. When they came, however, the shepherd boy told them it was just a mistake. He had only wanted company; there was no wolf. The villagers went home very angry, and the boy went back to his flock the next day.

SHEPHERD: *(Enters)* Gee, that alarm trick worked pretty well. Help came in only a few minutes. I wonder if I could do that again. Would they come as quickly a second time? I think I'll try it one more time. Here goes. *(Yells)* Wolf! Wolf! Come quickly to help! The wolf is after our flock! *(Exits)*

NARRATOR: One more time the villagers came to fight off the wolf, dropping whatever they were doing to come to the boy's aid. When they looked around, however, they realized that the boy had fooled them again. One by one, they scolded the shepherd for tricking them before they left for home.

SHEPHERD: *(Enters)* I don't know why, but these people have no sense of humor. It was only a joke, after all. What they were doing couldn't have been so important that they couldn't have afforded some time off. It was funny to see how serious they all were and how mad they were when they left. Ha, ha. Well, time to drive the flock back home. *(Exits)*

NARRATOR: The next day the shepherd drove his sheep one more time to the meadow.

SHEPHERD: *(Enters)* Even though that was fun to get the villagers out here, I don't think I should try it again—at least for a little while. They did seem awfully mad at me. Hey, what is that moving over there? *(Wolf enters)* Oh, no, I think I know. It's a wolf—a real wolf this time. What can I do? I'll just call out one more time for help. Even if they are mad, the villagers will come to help me. *(Yells)* Wolf! Wolf! Oh, help me! I'm not joking! There really is a wolf here this time! Help!!! *(Exits)*

NARRATOR: And do you know what happened? Absolutely nothing. The villagers just figured that the boy was fooling around one more time. They weren't about to be made fools of again. Well, it's not exactly true that nothing happened. The wolf ate all the sheep.

WOLF: *(Enters)* Yum, yum! *(Burps)* Pardon me. *(Exits)*

NARRATOR: The shepherd boy ran home as fast as he could to get help, but it was too late. All the sheep were gone. From that time on, the shepherd boy got a new name in the village. He was called "The Boy Who Cried 'Wolf.'" You know, after that, no one believed the shepherd boy ever again. I think that he would have been happy to have taken a flock out again to the meadow, even if it was boring, but he no longer was given the chance. Now when he calls out "Wolf," he no longer waits for the villagers to come. He just hopes the wolf will come back so that he has someone to talk to.

SHEPHERD: *(Enters)* Oh, Wolf! Wolf! Come back! Please come back!

The End

The Country Mouse and the City Mouse

Puppets needed:
    Country Mouse
    City Mouse

Prop:
    sack of food (optional)

NARRATOR: Once upon a time a simple country mouse invited her rich cousin who lived in the big city to visit her in her home in the country.

(Country Mouse and City Mouse enter)

COUNTRY MOUSE:

I'm so glad you could come to visit. Look at all the wonderful open space we have here in the country. We have such great freedom here. Fields as far as the eye can see filled with wheat and all the grains you could want. What more could any mouse wish for? All of this is ours for the taking. Ours is a simple life but, as you can see, a happy one.

CITY MOUSE:

I guess you do have a lot of wheat, but don't you get a little sick of eating the same thing for every meal?

COUNTRY MOUSE:

I don't know what you mean.

CITY MOUSE:

I guess I'm just used to a bit fancier food—more variety too. Nothing personal, mind you, but my house is much more nicely furnished also.

COUNTRY MOUSE:

I'm sorry you are disappointed with our home, but lots of families live quite happily here in the country.

CITY MOUSE:

I don't doubt that, Cousin, but have you ever been to the city? You probably don't know what you're missing. I'd like to have you as my guest for a week in the city. See then if you don't prefer city life to this. We dine like kings and queens in the city. We live in beautiful, richly furnished homes too. *(Both exit)*

NARRATOR: And so Country Mouse decided to see this great city life for herself. It did sound good. *(Both enter)*

COUNTRY MOUSE:

Thank you for inviting me to your place. This is quite a lovely home. Where do you and your family live in this mansion?

CITY MOUSE:

Actually we live in a place through that hole there in the floorboard. *(Points)*

COUNTRY MOUSE:

We have to squeeze through that hole?

CITY MOUSE:

Yes, but wait until you see the nice room through that hole. We have furnished it with the best things taken from the furnishings of this home.

COUNTRY MOUSE:

Oh, I'm sure it is lovely.

CITY MOUSE:

You must be hungry after your long trip here. Why don't I see what's in the kitchen for us to eat. There are always plenty of leftovers in the kitchen. *(Exits)*

NARRATOR:

So, City Mouse scampered up the table and carried away a little bit of all the leftovers.

CITY MOUSE:

(Enters with sack of food) Here's some chicken cooked in a fancy white sauce, some special cranberry sauce, some imported cheese, some fresh asparagus, and some lemon meringue pie for dessert.

COUNTRY MOUSE:

I've never seen such food in my life. It's almost too fancy to eat. Do you have food like this every day?

CITY MOUSE:

Most every day. Of course we have to be rather quick about getting the food off the table and about eating all this food.

COUNTRY MOUSE:

Why? I would like to enjoy these delicacies slowly.

CITY MOUSE:

Well, you see, we are not the only animals around here who live in the house.

COUNTRY MOUSE:

No? Who else lives here?

CITY MOUSE:

The people who own this house have a cat—a fairly large cat. He's not too friendly either.

COUNTRY MOUSE:

A cat? Oh, no! That sounds very dangerous.

CITY MOUSE:

Not if you are quick and always on your guard. You just have to be ready to run whenever you hear a "meow." Head for that hole there. The cat can't touch us if we squeeze through the hole. (Points)

COUNTRY MOUSE:

This will be a change for me. I guess I am used to eating as slowly as I like. I don't mind, though, because the food does look delicious.

NARRATOR: Just as the two mice started to nibble on their feast, they heard a frightening "meow!"

CITY MOUSE:

Quick, Cousin. Leave that food and run to the hole. We'll eat later.

NARRATOR: And they both raced for the hole. (Both run to other side of stage)

COUNTRY MOUSE:

You know, Cousin, I appreciate your hospitality, but I think I'll head back home to the country this afternoon. You may have delicious food and live in a great house, but I think I will stick with my wheat fields. Mine may not be as fancy a life, but it's surely more pleasant and peaceful. Bye, Cousin, and thanks for your hospitality. Come and visit me in the country whenever you get tired of this hectic city life. (Exits)

CITY MOUSE:

(Calls after) Bye, bye, Cousin. (Shrugs. Says to himself) I guess there's no accounting for taste.

NARRATOR: Moral: sometimes a simple life that is secure and safe is more enjoyable than a rich and lavish life that is filled with danger.

The End

The Dog and the Wolf

Puppets needed:
　　Dog
　　Wolf

Props:
　　none

NARRATOR: Once upon a time poor Wolf was cold and hungry, roaming around the woods. He wandered here and there looking for a warm cave to hide in and a meal to fill up his empty stomach. As he wandered in the dark, he came upon a cabin at the outskirts of the woods. A dog was outside in the backyard. As he passed by the yard, the dog barked out to him in a friendly tone. *(Dog and Wolf enter)*

DOG: Hello to you, Cousin Wolf. Please come in the yard and stay awhile.

WOLF: Greetings to you, friend Dog. Thank you for your invitation, for it is a very cold night. I could use a warm place to stay and a hearty meal. But what about your master? Surely he will not let me come in.

DOG: My master will not care. He rarely questions me on those who come into the yard.

WOLF: It is kind of you to offer me shelter.

DOG: Oh, it is not kindness alone that prompts me to let you in. I would like a companion to sit with me and tell me about how it used to be when dogs roamed freely. Some nights are long and lonely for me. Sometimes the master is not here at all at night, and some other nights I must keep my master amused and happy, even when I am in a bad mood.

WOLF: Hmm . . . And what are you required to do for the master?

DOG: Oh, not much really. Of course I have to guard the house against anyone who would come in. I must be on guard all day and night.

WOLF: I could help with that. I can be very fierce looking and sounding.

DOG: I'll bet. And then I have to fetch the paper in every morning for the master to read.

WOLF: Seems easy enough. What else?

DOG: Not much. Well, of course, I also guard the chicken coop to see that all of the chickens are well and safe.

WOLF: I could surely do that for you. I'm good with chickens. Master wouldn't mind if I took a small snack once in a while from the coop, would he?

DOG: Oh, yes. No snacking. All the chickens and eggs have to be accounted for. Master likes an omelet very morning, and once a week he eats a chicken for his dinner.

WOLF: He eats a chicken for dinner. But what about you?

DOG: Oh, don't worry about me. I get to have any chicken scraps that are left over at the end of the week. Of course there's usually not much left after Master has eaten. He likes his chicken.

WOLF: And what do you do when he eats his meals?

DOG: Why I look at him, of course, and wait to see if any scraps fall to the floor while he is eating.

WOLF: Are you allowed to sneak a few bites of food if Master isn't looking?

DOG: Oh, no! I have to stay low on the floor and never jump up to the table.

WOLF: Hmm . . .

DOG: But I do have my own food dish, which the master fills every evening for me.

WOLF: That sounds good. Is it filled with fresh meat every day?

DOG: Well, not really meat. The master has a big bag of dry food that he pours into the dish every day. It has a kind of meat flavor.

WOLF: Yuck! Dry food—that doesn't sound too appetizing.

DOG: Oh, you get used to it. Not much variety, though. It is filling. That's the main thing. Of course after eating you have to accompany Master each night for a long walk. That's always a good part of the night.

WOLF: I could do that. I love to wander freely at night—just exploring.

DOG: You wouldn't be wandering freely, I'm afraid.

WOLF: No? What do you mean?

DOG: Well, Master insists I wear this leather collar on my neck and that is attached to a long metal chain he calls a leash. You have to bring it to him at night so that he can attach it to the leather collar before we go on the walk.

WOLF: Is that why part of your neck fur looks a bit worn away?

DOG: I guess so. The collar does tend to rub a bit. It doesn't hurt, though. You'll soon get used to it. You just have to be sure to walk at the same speed the master walks, or your neck might get a little bit sore from the leash yanking on it.

WOLF: Ouch! But you get to run about the yard freely during the day, don't you?

DOG: Well, usually when Master isn't at home, I am chained outside in the yard.

WOLF:	Chained up?
DOG:	The master couldn't have me running about and getting in trouble, could he?
WOLF:	You know, Dog, I thank you kindly for your offer of shelter, but I think your work is just too hard for me. I couldn't take it.
DOG:	But . . . ?
WOLF:	I'd rather have my freedom and be hungry than be fed and be a slave to Master. Thanks, but no thanks. See you, friend Dog. *(Exits)*
NARRATOR:	And so Wolf trotted off back into the woods with a smile on his face and his tail held high. And Dog? Well, Dog got ready for his evening of being a night watchdog.
DOG:	Poor unfortunate Wolf. Some of us just don't have what it takes, I guess. My dogged dedication just isn't for everyone. *(Calls out)* Well, bye, Wolf. See you around.
NARRATOR:	I guess the moral of this story is that a dog's life is not for everyone!
WOLF:	*(Pokes head in)* Especially not for a wolf like me!

The End

The Fox and the Cat

Puppets needed:
  Fox
  Cat

Props:
  none

NARRATOR: One day Fox and his friend Cat were talking together. Fox was bragging about his ability to escape from any situation and trying to impress Cat with his great cleverness.

(Cat and Fox enter)

FOX: That's one thing about me. I can get away from any enemy. It isn't because I am the swiftest animal of the forest. It's because I am so clever. I just have to decide on one of the many ways I can use to escape. I think I have about 100 or more ways to trick those hunting dogs that come sniffing around. I bet you don't have that many tricks up your sleeve, huh, Cat?

CAT: Me, no, I have one plan of escape and one only. I must say, though, that one means of escape is all I ever needed.

FOX: Well, if you only have one, that's OK. Stick with that one way for you. Not everyone is as clever as a fox at using his wits to plan escapes.

NARRATOR: Suddenly both Cat and Fox heard the yelps and cries of a pack of hunting hounds heading right toward them. *(Yelp and bark)*

CAT: I know what I am going to do. Works every time. I will climb up the nearest tree as quickly as I can. If I climb high enough, I won't be seen from the ground.

FOX: Can't you come up with a more clever plan?

CAT: What about you, Fox? How are you going to escape from those hounds? They sound like they are getting close. You had better be quick in making up your mind.

FOX: Well, I could run the hounds around in a circle. I like that trick. Tires them out. It's funny to see those dogs running around with their tongues hanging out. I've used that a few times. Then there's the one in which I run right straight to the den. The hounds can't fit in the den, and they can't even find the entrance. They get really frustrated with that one. Then there's the one in which I try to throw the hounds off by wearing a lambskin coat. Oh, there are so many of my clever tricks. There's also the one in which I . . .

CAT: Just choose one quickly, Fox. I have got to go now. I'm climbing that tree over there. *(Exits)*

FOX: I could do something simple like that, but as I said, it's just not clever enough for my tastes and abilities.

NARRATOR: Soon the hounds were getting nearer and nearer. Fox just couldn't make up his mind. All his plans amused him. Finally the hounds got very close. They were right upon him. Cat couldn't stand it any longer. She looked down and saw Fox just standing around thinking. She climbed down the tree and meowed as loudly as she could. *(Cat climbs up the back of stage; meows)* It was enough to throw the hounds off the track of Fox and on to the track of Cat. Then as quickly as she could, she scampered up another tree. *(Cat exits)* Later that day Fox met Cat again.

CAT: *(Enters)* Well, did you get away in one piece from all those hounds, Fox?

FOX: Yes, I was fine. You never have to worry about me. Of course I am so clever that those old hounds will never catch me. I do thank you for your efforts to distract the pack. It was a nice thing for you to do, even if I didn't need the help. Want to hear about my successful escape this last time?

CAT: You know, I think I have heard enough. I will continue to use my one safe means of escape. It works even if it's not all that clever. Sometimes you are too clever for your own good, Fox.

FOX: Oh, you are joking, Cat. How can I be too clever?

NARRATOR: Poor Fox never did learn his lesson, but the moral of this tale is that it is better to know one safe, sure way to do something than to imagine 100 clever ways that may or may not work.

The End

The Hare and the Tortoise

Puppets needed:

Hare

Tortoise

Props:

NARRATOR: Once upon a time there was a hare who loved to brag about himself to anyone who would listen. He would brag about his cleverness, his exceptional good looks, his great strength, and especially his speed.

(Tortoise and Hare enter)

HARE: I am the fastest rabbit in the whole county—maybe even in the whole state. Of course I have already won many races, but I should find another race I can enter so that I can show everyone how fast a rabbit can be.

NARRATOR: Well, it so happened that there was a tortoise that heard the hare's boasting and was sick of listening to all the bragging. Finally the tortoise couldn't stand it anymore and spoke up.

TORTOISE: Listen here, Hare, we are all tired of hearing your boasting. You may run very fast, but surely you are not the swiftest runner around here.

HARE: Well, now, the little Tortoise thinks I am just bragging about being such a good runner. How about you, Tortoise, want to challenge me yourself? Ha, ha, what a joke! Too bad your legs are so short and slow. Not much to compare with my fine long legs, huh?

TORTOISE: I think I will take you up on your offer, Hare. I will bet you that I can win a race with you any day that you choose.

HARE: Are you serious? You are known to be one of the slowest-moving animals around. Challenge me? You know I will be sure to win.

TORTOISE: You never know.

(Hare exits)

NARRATOR: And so a race was agreed on, and Tortoise started in immediately on a training schedule to get ready for the race.

TORTOISE: *(Does some exercises)* First I will do some push-ups to get in shape for running, and then I will start to jog every day—going a little bit further and longer every time.

NARRATOR: But Hare didn't bother with any training. He was confident that he could win without even trying.

HARE: *(Enters)* This race is going to be a piece of cake. How can I lose? I surely don't need to do any preparation for this race.

(Both Hare and Tortoise exit)

NARRATOR: And so the hare did no exercise at all to get in condition; instead, he decided to take it very easy. He ate well and relaxed. Soon the day of the big race was here. All the animals in the area came to watch the hare win another race. Finally the race began, and both the hare and the tortoise took off. Hare took off in a flash, and Tortoise, well, Tortoise took off as quickly as he could on his short legs. Hare left poor Tortoise in the dust.

(Tortoise and Hare enter)

HARE: This race shouldn't take too long. I'd like to be done soon so I can have dinner. *(Moves across stage)* How about it, Tortoise, do you give up yet? Oh, Tortoise, are you still there? Can you hear me? Ha, ha.

TORTOISE: I'm still here. I may not be the swiftest animal around, but I don't give up. *(Exits)*

HARE: I am so far ahead as it is that I think I'll stop for a quick breakfast. I think I'll eat some carrots and lettuce and rest up in the field.
(Lies down)

NARRATOR: And as Hare ate and rested in the field, Tortoise kept up a slow but steady pace. Still there was a great distance between the hare and the tortoise.

HARE: That was a good light meal and I am really full. Now I feel like a nice short nap. I can't run on a full stomach, after all.

NARRATOR: Hare settled down and sang a song to relax.

HARE: *(Sings to the tune of "Frère Jacques")*

> I'm a winner; I'm a winner.
> I can't lose; I can't lose.
> I'm so far ahead now. I'm so far ahead now.
> I'll just snooze. I'll just snooze. *(Snores)*

NARRATOR: And Hare settled in for a short rest. He wanted to sleep just for a short time, but he was really tired. You see, he had stayed up late the night before going to a big celebration victory party. What was supposed to be a short nap turned into a long period of sleep—one hour, then two, and finally three hours. Suddenly Hare awoke with a start.

HARE: I think I hear voices cheering. Why are they doing that? I haven't finished the race yet. They don't have to cheer for me yet. Well, I think I'll get up and run to the finish line to accept my prize.

NARRATOR: When Hare got to the finish line, guess what he saw? Tortoise was accepting the prize for being the winner of the race.

HARE: This is ridiculous. You can't beat me! I'm the swiftest runner of them all. I demand a rematch.

NARRATOR: But Hare's words were drowned out by the cheering of the crowd. "Hooray for Tortoise!" "The winner!" Tortoise modestly accepted the crowd's cheers.

TORTOISE: (*Enters*) Thank you all. I may not be the swiftest, fastest animal, but I won anyway. I just didn't give up. I'm glad I trained so hard for the race. It really paid off.

NARRATOR: For his acceptance speech Tortoise sang this song.

TORTOISE: (*Sings to the tune of "Row, Row, Row Your Boat"*)

> Slowly wins the race.
> I will not give in.
> Steadily, steadily, steadily, steadily,
> Try your best to win.

NARRATOR: And what about Hare? He decided all this activity made him tired again. He needed another short nap.

HARE: Ho, hum, silly little race. Just won by a fluke—all a mistake. No sense getting too upset by all of this, but I do think I need another short rest. (*Snores*)

NARRATOR: One moral of this story is that bragging alone won't win a race. Hard work and steady progress is more likely to make a winner.

TORTOISE: (*Sings to the tune of "Row, Row, Row Your Boat"*)

> Steadily, steadily, steadily, steadily,
> Try your best to win.

The End

Part Three APPENDIXES

Songs and Parodies to Use

Appendix A

*H*ere are some suggestions for children's songs to use during intermissions between scripts. You can easily get the complete lyrics on the Internet if you don't have the sheet music for them, or you can find the music and lyrics in good anthologies of children's songs. For variety, consider writing parodies to these well-known melodies, or use some of the original parodies that follow.

SONGS TO SING

"Aiken Drum"

"B-I-N-G-O"

"Clementine"

"Dem Bones"

"Farmer in the Dell"

"Frère Jacques"

"Frosty the Snowman"

"Here Comes Santa Claus"

"Hokey Pokey"

"If You're Happy and You Know It"

"I've Been Working on the Railroad"

"Jingle Bells"

"Oh, Susannah"

"Old MacDonald Had a Farm"

"On Top of Old Smoky"

"Pop Goes the Weasel"

"Put Your Finger in the Air"

"Row, Row, Row Your Boat"

"Rudolph the Red-Nosed Reindeer"

"She'll Be Coming 'Round the Mountain"

"Shortnin' Bread"

"Skip to My Lou"

"There's a Hole in the Bottom of the Sea"

"Three Blind Mice"

"Up on the Housetop"

"Wheels on the Bus"

SOME PARODIES TO USE WITH FAMILIAR MELODIES

TO THE TUNE OF "SHE'LL BE COMING 'ROUND THE MOUNTAIN," YOU CAN ADD THESE VERSES:

1. She'll be reading *Harry Potter* when she comes—turn the page!
2. She'll be talking on the cell phone when she comes—shut it off!
3. She'll be heading to the library when she comes—charge out!
4. She'll be listening to a DiscMan when she comes—turn it down!
5. She'll be enjoying summer weather when she comes—whew! It's hot!

(Change the following for the season)

Fall: She'll be going trick-or-treating when she comes—sugar high!

Winter: She'll be trudging through a snowstorm when she comes—brr! It's cold!

Spring: She'll be eating Easter candy when she comes—yum, yum!

Summer: She'll be driving through a heat wave when she comes—cool down!

"DINO" (SUNG TO THE TUNE OF "B-I-N-G-O"—FOR THOSE GOOD WITH TONGUE TWISTERS)

There was a scientist had a dinosaur, and Allosaurus was his name-o.
A-L-L-O-S-A-U-R-U-S, A-L-L-O-S-A-U-R-U-S, A-L-L-O-S-A-U-R-U-S, and Allosaurus was his name-o.

Well, Allosaurus was afraid of water, so the scientist found another beast-o.
B-R-O-N-T-O-S-A-U-R-U-S, B-R-O-N-T-O-S-A-U-R-U-S, B-R-O-N-T-O-S-A-U-R-U-S, and Brontosaurus was his name-o.

This Brontosaurus was none too bright; his brain was the size of a nut-o.
Poor B-R-O-N-T-O-S-A-U-R-U-S, B-R-O-N-T-O-S-A-U-R-U-S, B-R-O-N-T-O-S-A-U-R-U-S, with a brain the size of a nut-o.

Another dinosaur joined the group, and he looked just like a duck-o.
T-R-A-C-H-O-D-O-N, T-R-A-C-H-O-D-O-N, T-R-A-C-H-O-D-O-N; he looked just like a duck-o.

That Trachodon liked water too much, so the scientist bought another.
T-R-I-C-E-R-A-T-O-P-S, T-R-I-C-E-R-A-T-O-P-S, T-R-I-C-E-R-A-T-O-P-S, and Triceratops was his name-o.

Well, Triceratops fought all the time; his temper was so mean-o.
T-R-I-C-E-R-A-T-O-P-S, T-R-I-C-E-R-A-T-O-P-S, T-R-I-C-E-R-A-T-O-P-S; his temper was so mean-o.

So the scientist hired himself a foreman, and Tyrannosaurus Rex was his name-o.
T-Y-R-A-N-N-O-S-A-U-R-U-S R-E-X, T-Y-R-A-N-N-O-S-A-U-R-U-S R-E-X, T-Y-R-A-N-N-O-S-A-U-R-U-S R-E-X, and T-Rex was his name-o.

Now there's no question who's master there; there surely is no doubt-o.
T-Y-R-A-N-N-O-S-A-U-R-U-S R-E-X, T-Y-R-A-N-N-O-S-A-U-R-U-S R-E-X,
T-Y-R-A-N-N-O-S-A-U-R-U-S R-E-X, and T-Rex was his name-o!

"WHEN TYRANNOSAURUS REX COMES TOWERING IN"
(SUNG TO THE TUNE OF "WHEN THE SAINTS COME MARCHING IN")

Oh, when that Allosaurus comes walking in,
Oh, when that Allosaurus comes walking in,
Boy, I'd love to be in that number,
When that Allosaurus comes walking in.

Oh, when that Trachodon comes waddling in,
Oh, when that Trachodon comes waddling in,
Boy, I'd love to be in that number,
When that Trachodon comes waddling in.

Oh, when Corythosaurus comes swimming in,
Oh, when Corythosaurus comes swimming in,
Boy, I'd love to be in that number,
When Corythosaurus comes swimming in.

Oh, when Stegosaurus comes blundering in,
Oh, when Stegosaurus comes blundering in,
Boy, I'd love to be in that number,
When Stegosaurus comes blundering in.

Oh, when Brontosaurus comes thundering in,
Oh, when Brontosaurus comes thundering in,
Boy, I'd love to be in that number,
When Brontosaurus comes thundering in.

Oh, when Triceratops comes thrusting in,
Oh, when Triceratops comes thrusting in,
Boy, I'd love to be in that number,
When Triceratops comes thrusting in.

Oh, when Tyrannosaurus Rex comes towering in,
Oh, when Tyrannosaurus Rex comes towering in,
That's when I'd get out of that number,
When Tyrannosaurus Rex comes towering in!

"IT'S HALLOWEEN"
(SUNG TO THE TUNE OF "THREE BLIND MICE")

Halloween. Halloween.
It's lot's of fun. It's lots of fun.
We knock at some doors and yell, "Trick-or-treat."
We fill up our bags with good things to eat.
Did you ever see more tasty sweets?
It's Halloween. Halloween.

Halloween. Halloween.
My favorite night. My favorite night.
We dress up in costumes and look so fine.
There's candy for you, and the rest is mine.
So better get ready. It's almost time!
It's Halloween. Halloween.

"I'VE BEEN WAITING FOR THANKSGIVING"
(SUNG TO THE TUNE OF "I'VE BEEN WORKING ON THE RAILROAD")

I've been waiting for Thanksgiving,
All the live-long day.
I've been helping in the kitchen,
Just to pass the time away.
Can't you hear our stomachs grumbling?
Table's already set.
Can't you hear the family mumbling,
"Turkey's not done yet"?

Daddy won't you carve,
Daddy won't you carve,
Daddy won't you carve that bi—rd?
Momma won't you serve,
Momma won't you serve,
Momma won't you serve that bird?

Someone's in the kitchen with Momma.
Someone's in the kitchen, I know, oh, oh, oh.
Someone's in the kitchen with Momma,
Gnawing on a drumstick bone.
And singing, "Fee, fie, fiddle-e-i-o,
Fee, fie, fiddle-e-i-o, oh, oh, oh.
Fee, fie, fiddle-e-i-o,"
Gnawing on a drumstick bone!

Appendix B

Using a Large Puppet to Introduce Puppet Plays

Sometimes it is useful to have a large body puppet introduce the shows as a kind of emcee. For this large puppet, you may be able to place your hand and part of your arm in the puppet. Here's an example of how you might use a dinosaur puppet as an emcee for a Christmas show.

Dinosaur Christmas Emcee

DINOSAUR: *(You might put a Santa hat on him)* Hello, boys and girls. My name is Santasaurus Rex, but you can call me Santa Rex. I lived about 144 million years ago, but I'm visiting today to get us all in a holiday mood. I bet you all have heard of Christmas trees and think that dinosaurs have nothing to do with Christmas, but that's where you're wrong. It all started about 225 million years ago in the late Triassic period when my dinosaur ancestors that ate plants lived on the earth. One day Mrs. Plateosaur was planning a special banquet at her place to celebrate the New Year when she had an idea. You see, Mr. and Mrs. Plateosaur were conifer-eating dinosaurs—they loved to eat pine trees and those pinecones.

Yummy! Well, Mrs. Plateosaur thought that instead of inviting other dinosaurs over to their part of the woods, she would bring a nice-sized pine tree over to their place. They could all eat a good meal—family style at home. She found a nice, fresh, juicy tree and lugged it home, but it looked so pretty when she got it home that the family just wanted to look at it, not eat it. This, you see, was the first official Christmas tree, and we dinosaurs had it. Of course my ancestors did eat the tree eventually at their party. It was just too delicious to waste. So, when you see a pretty Christmas tree, think of my ancestor, Mrs. Plateosaur, who brought the first Christmas tree in for Christmas dinner. *(Pause, as if reflecting)* Well, you are right. I guess I prefer a good steak too. So much for thinking of food. How about a puppet show today, starring some of my other favorite puppet friends? Our first show is . . ."

(At the end of the shows, you might
bring the dinosaur puppet out again to say good-bye)

Dinosaur: Good-bye, boys and girls. I hope that we gave all of you some holiday spirit. And you remember my ancestor, Mrs. Plateosaur, when you light up your Christmas tree. Say, wait a minute, let's dedicate one last song to Mrs. Plateosaur. Without her, after all, we might not have our beautiful Christmas trees. How about joining me in singing "We Wish You a Merry Christmas"?

Using Puppets to Tell Jokes and Riddles

Appendix C

Any experienced children's librarian knows that some of the most worn books in the collection are the joke and riddle books. Children love humor that they can understand.

You can capitalize on this by having a large puppet tell some jokes and riddles in an intermission between puppet scripts. Use an appropriate animal for the puppet show. For spring shows, for example, you could use a rabbit or a frog puppet to tell rabbit or frog riddles and jokes. You can find riddles appropriate for almost any animal by searching in Google under "rabbit riddles" or "frog riddles" and so forth. Pick three or four of the funniest riddles you find. Let the puppet ask the riddle, and give the audience a little time to think of an answer.

You can also find some good books with jokes and riddles to use between your shows. Here are a few I recommend:

Hall, Katy, and Lisa Eisenberg. *Buggy Riddles*. New York: Dial, 1986.
———. *Bunny Riddles*. New York: Dial, 1998.
———. *Chickie Riddles*. New York: Dial, 1998.
———. *Creepy Riddles*. New York: Dial, 1998.
———. *Dino Riddles*. New York: Dial, 2002.
———. *Fishy Riddles*. New York: Dial, 1986.
———. *Grizzly Riddles*. New York: Dial, 1989.
———. *Kitty Riddles*. New York: Dial, 2000.
———. *Mummy Riddles*. New York: Dial, 1997.
———. *Puppy Riddles*. New York: Dial, 1998.
———. *Sheepish Riddles*. New York: Dial, 1996.

————. *Snakey Riddles*. New York: Dial, 1990.

Keller, Charles. *Count Draculations: Monster Riddles*. Niles, Ill.: Prentice-Hall, 1986.

Most, Bernard. *Zoodles*. New York: Harcourt, 1992.

Phillips, Louis. *Wackysaurus*. New York: Viking, 1991.

Roop, Peter, and Connie Roop. *Let's Celebrate! Jokes about Holidays*. Minneapolis: Lerner, 1986.

Rosenbloom, Joseph. *The Funniest Dinosaur Book Ever!* New York: Sterling, 1987.

Saurus, Alice. *1,001 Dinosaur Jokes*. New York: Ballantine, 1993.

Seltzer, Meyer. *Hide and Go Shriek Monster Riddles*. Niles, Ill.: Albert Whitman, 1990.

Sources of Poetry to Perform with Puppets

Appendix D

Almost any good anthology of children's poetry will provide you with many examples of poetry that you might use as entertainments between the puppet scripts. Either you can read the poem as the narrator or you can use one of your animal puppets (appropriate to the poem) to read the poem. You might use a large dinosaur puppet, for example, to read or act out one of the many poems about monsters in John Foster's *Dragons, Dinosaurs, and Monster Poems* (Oxford: Oxford Univ. Pr., 1998).

The Random House Book of Poetry for Children (New York: Random, 1984), edited by Jack Prelutsky, affords many poems to use on many different subjects. Here are some poems you might read from this anthology:

For a spring show—use "April Rain Song" by Langston Hughes or "The Tree Frog" by John Travers Moore

For Halloween—use "This Is Halloween" by Dorothy Brown Thompson or "Lazy Witch" by Myra Cohn Livingston

For Thanksgiving—use "Thanksgiving" by Ivy O. Eastwick

For winter—use "Read This with Gestures" by John Ciardi or "Grandpa Bear's Lullaby" by Jane Yolen

For Christmas—use "The Donkey" (anonymous)

For Valentine's Day—use "Valentine" by Shel Silverstein

For a library theme—use "The Library" by Barbara A. Huff

With a shark puppet—use "The Shark" by Lord Alfred Douglas

With a cow puppet—use "The Cow" by Jack Prelutsky

For a boy or girl puppet—use "Wrong Start" by Marchette Chute or "Mother Doesn't Want a Dog" by Judith Viorst

Another anthology edited by Jack Prelutsky, *Read-Aloud Rhymes for the Very Young* (New York: Knopf, 1986), has a number of poems that could be performed by a puppet narrator:

> *For a spring show*—use "Mud" by Polly Chase Boyden
> or "The Toad" by Elizabeth Coatsworth
> or "The Spring Wind" by Charlotte Zolotow
> or "Pussy Willows" by Aileen Fisher
> or "Squirrel in the Rain" by Frances Frost
>
> *For a winter show*—use "The More It Snows" by A. A. Milne
> or "The Mitten Song" by Marie Louise Allen
> or "Jack Frost" by Helen Bayley Davis
>
> *With a cat puppet*—use "Cat Kisses" by Bobbi Katz
>
> *With a fish puppet*—use "Wish" by Dorothy Brown Thompson
>
> *With a dinosaur puppet*—use "Unfortunately" by Bobbi Katz
>
> *For any show*—use "Tell Me, Little Woodworm" by Spike Milligan
> or "Sneeze" by Maxine Kumin

From Jack Prelutsky's *Something Big Has Been Here* (New York: Greenwillow, 1998), use a puppet to act out these poems:

> *With a boy or girl puppet*—use "I Know All the Sounds That the Animals Make"
>
> *With a boy or girl puppet*—use "Turkey Shot Out of the Oven"
>
> *With a pig puppet*—use "You're Eating Like a Pig Again"
>
> *With a dog puppet*—use "Hello! How Are You? I Am Fine"
>
> *With a boy or girl puppet*—use "Mosquitoes, Mosquitoes"
>
> *With a dinosaur puppet*—use "I Saw a Brontosaurus"

From Jeff Moss's *The Butterfly Jar* (New York: Bantam, 1989), choose one or more of these poems:

> *With a butterfly puppet*—use "Butterfly Jar"
>
> *With a boy puppet and a girl puppet*—use "If I Had a Penny"
>
> *With a boy puppet*—use "The Monster"
>
> *With a dinosaur puppet*—use "Brontosaurus"
>
> *With any puppet*—use "Possible Confusion"
>
> *With any puppet*—use "Purple"
>
> *With any puppet*—use "Bugs"

From *Talking Like the Rain* (New York: Little, Brown, 1992), edited by X. J. Kennedy, you might use one of these poems:

> *With a girl puppet and a monster puppet*—use "I Eat Kids. Yum Yum!" by Dennis Lee
>
> *With a chicken or a child puppet*—use "The Chicken" (anonymous)
>
> *With a child puppet*—use "Cat" by Mary Britton Miller
>
> *With a cow puppet*—use "The Cow" by Robert Louis Stevenson
>
> *With a polar bear puppet*—use "Polar Bear" by William Jay Smith
>
> *With a wolf puppet*—use "The Wolf" by Georgia Roberts Durston
>
> *With a witch puppet*—use "The Witches' Ride" by Karla Kuskin

 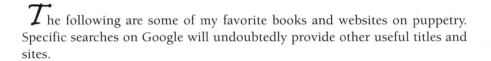

Appendix E

Some Good Books and Websites on Puppetry

*T*he following are some of my favorite books and websites on puppetry. Specific searches on Google will undoubtedly provide other useful titles and sites.

BOOKS

Adair, Margaret Weeks. *Do-It-in-a-Day: Puppets for Beginners*. New York: John Day, 1964.

Includes patterns for easy-to-make puppets.

Adair, Margaret Weeks, and Elizabeth Patapoff. *Folk Puppet Plays for the Social Studies*. New York: John Day, 1972.

Contains several play scripts for multiple puppeteers.

Andersen, Penny. *Let's Start a Puppet Theatre*. New York: Van Nostrand Reinhold, 1971.

Includes directions for making all types of puppets and stages.

Anderson, Dee. *Amazingly Easy Puppet Plays*. Chicago: American Library Assn., 1996.

Offers advice on getting started plus many easy original scripts for shows—also good bibliographies for sources and suppliers of materials.

Bany-Winters, Lisa. *On Stage: Theater Games and Activities for Kids*. Chicago: Chicago Review, 1997.

Includes great warm-up exercises and dramatic icebreakers—would be a good text for a beginning drama group.

Batchelder, Marjorie. *The Puppet Theatre Handbook*. New York: Harper and Brothers, 1947.

Provides plans and patterns for puppets and wooden stages.

Bauer, Caroline Feller. *Leading Kids to Books through Puppets*. Chicago: American Library Assn., 1997.

Shows various easy ways to create and use puppets.

Beresford, Margaret. *How to Make Puppets and Teach Puppetry*. New York: Taplinger, 1966.

Provides good directions for puppet construction, including papier-mâché puppet heads—also scripts with multiple characters.

Boylan, Eleanor. *How to Be a Puppeteer*. New York: McCall, 1970.

Gives a good introduction to traditional puppet performances.

Champlain, Connie. *Storytelling with Puppets*. Chicago: American Library Assn., 1998.

Shows how storytelling can be enriched with the use of puppets; includes reasons for using and methods of using puppets effectively.

Chernoff, Goldi Taub. *Puppet Party*. New York: Walker, 1971.

Good for younger puppet performers on puppet construction.

Currell, David. *An Introduction to Puppets and Puppet-Making*. Edison, N.J.: Chartwell, 1996.

Offers how-to instructions for making all kinds of puppets and some types of stages.

Engler, Larry, and Carol Fijan. *Making Puppets Come Alive: How to Learn and Teach Puppetry*. Mineola, N.Y.: Dover, 1973.

Two respected names in puppetry offer advice on gestures, posture, movements, and voices of puppets.

Fijan, Carol, and Frank Ballard. *Directing Puppet Theatre*. San Jose, Calif.: Resource Pubs., 1989.

Explains the director's role in every aspect of puppetry.

Hanford, Robert Ten Eyck. *The Complete Book of Puppetry and Puppeteering*. New York: Drake, 1976.

Includes the history of puppets and tips from professional puppeteers.

Howard, Vernon. *Puppet and Pantomime Plays*. New York: Sterling, 1963.

Includes good ideas for writing scripts.

Hunt, Tamara. *Pocketful of Puppets: Never Pick a Python for a Pet.* Austin, Tex.: Nancy Renfro Studios, 1984.

Animal poems and puppet patterns and activities.

Hunt, Tamara, and Nancy Renfro. *Pocketful of Puppets: Mother Goose.* Austin, Tex.: Nancy Renfro Studios, 1982.

One of the Pocketful of Puppet series of books, with patterns and ideas for puppetry.

Jenkins, Peggy Davison. *The Magic of Puppetry: A Guide for Those Working with Young Children.* Englewood Cliffs, N.J.: Prentice-Hall, 1980.

Includes discussion of the value of using puppetry, techniques, puppet making, and staging.

Jones, Taffy. *Whistle Stop Puppet Plays.* London: McFarland, 1983.

Includes several puppet plays for multiple children to perform.

MacLennan, Jennifer. *Simple Puppets You Can Make.* New York: Sterling, 1988.

Wonderfully detailed patterns for all sorts of human and animal puppets.

Minkel, Walter. *How to Do "The Three Little Bears" with Two Hands.* Chicago: American Library Assn., 2000.

Detailed advice on techniques, script writing or adapting, and staging shows; includes some scripts for multiple characters.

Moloney, Joan. *Making Puppets and Puppet Theatres.* New York: Frederick Fell, 1973.

Directions for puppets made from all sorts of materials from wood to fabric and tissue paper. Includes how to string marionettes and information on how to make various types of theaters.

Philpott, A. R. *Eight Plays for Hand Puppets.* Boston: Plays, 1968.

Includes good puppetry advice as well as eight play scripts that use multiple puppeteers.

Ross, Laura. *Hand Puppets: How to Make and Use Them.* New York: Lothrop, Lee and Shepard, 1969.

Advice on making papier-mâché and other types of puppets.

————. *Holiday Puppets.* New York: Lothrop, Lee and Shepard, 1974.

Includes good holiday scripts for multiple-character shows.

————. *Puppet Show Using Poems and Stories*. New York: Lothrop, Lee and Shepard, 1970.

Offers many good examples of story lines and poetry for performance.

Rump, Nan. *Puppets and Masks: Stagecraft and Storytelling*. Worcester, Mass.: Davis Pubs., 1996.

Emphasizes classroom and large group use of puppetry; includes good instructions for making all types of puppets and for students to develop performance skills. Also included are scripts for class performances of folktales from different countries.

Schramm, Toni A. *Puppet Plays: From Workshop to Performance*. Englewood, Colo.: Teacher Ideas Pr., 1993.

Contains good, easy puppet patterns; advice on how to conduct workshops for children in puppetry; and several ready-to-perform, original puppet scripts for groups.

Sierra, Judy. *Puppets for Dreaming and Scheming*. Walnut Creek, Calif.: Early Stages, 1978.

Includes easy puppet scripts and simple puppet patterns.

VanSchuyver, Jan. *Storytelling Made Easy with Puppets*. Phoenix, Ariz.: Oryx, 1993.

Offers excellent hints for beginning storytellers on types of stories to tell and the ways adults and students can use puppets to tell stories more effectively.

Winer, Yvonne. *Pocketful of Puppets: Three Plump Fish*. Austin, Tex.: Nancy Renfro Studios, 1983.

Contains story and pattern ideas.

Wright, Denise Anton. *One-Person Puppet Plays*. Englewood, Colo.: Teacher Ideas Pr., 1990.

Includes many scripts with multiple characters and patterns for puppets.

WEBSITES ON PUPPETS

http://sagecraft.com/puppetry/using/index.html

http://sunniebunniezz.com/puppetry/puppet.htm

Yvonne Amar Frey has worked as a school librarian for the past fourteen years in Peoria (Ill.) District 150—as a regional librarian and library supervisor for thirteen years, and currently as the librarian at Richwoods High School. Prior to working in the school venue, she was the head of youth services at the Peoria Public Library's main building, where she got her start in puppetry. In addition, Frey has taught children's literature at the junior college level and English literature and composition at the high school and university levels. She received a master's degree in literature from Johns Hopkins University in Baltimore, under a Woodrow Wilson Scholarship, and a master's of arts in library science degree from Rosary College in River Forest, Illinois. She has been awarded National Endowment for the Humanities Fellowships in literature in the summers of 2001 and 2004. She is serving for a second term as a member of the Alliance Library System board of directors in East Peoria. She has performed, written scripts for, and made puppets and stages for puppet shows for almost twenty years.